To Preserve the Republic

To Preserve the Republic

Two Histories of Union Infantry Companies
during the American Civil War

Company F,
1st Regiment
Rhode Island Volunteers
Charles H. Clarke

Company E,
6th Minnesota Regiment
of Volunteer Infantry
Alfred J. Hill

LEONAUR

To Preserve the Republic
Two Histories of Union Infantry Companies
during the American Civil War
Company F, 1st Regiment
Rhode Island Volunteers by Charles H. Clarke
Company E, 6th Minnesota Regiment
of Volunteer Infantry by Alfred J. Hill

First published under the titles

History of Company F, 1st Regiment
Rhode Island Volunteers
and
History of Company E of the 6th Minnesota Regiment
of Volunteer Infantry

Leonaur is an imprint of Oakpast Ltd

Copyright in this form © 2010 Oakpast Ltd

ISBN: 978-0-85706-106-5 (hardcover)
ISBN: 978-0-85706-105-8 (softcover)

http://www.leonaur.com

Publisher's Notes

In the interests of authenticity, the spellings, grammar and place names
used have been retained from the original editions.

The opinions of the authors represent a view of events in which he
was a participant related from his own perspective,
as such the text is relevant as an historical document.

The views expressed in this book are not necessarily
those of the publisher.

Contents

Company F,
1st Regiment
Rhode Island Volunteers

Charles H. Clarke

Contents

Introduction

In the following pages I have endeavoured to present a correct description of the service performed by Company F, 1st Regiment R. I. Volunteers, during the spring and summer of 1861. While many of my comrades who served in that company may differ with me in some of the statements I have made, still I think that all will agree that what I have presented is as correct an account as can be had at this late period of that service. Thirty years is a long time for men to remember the particulars of any event, unless some memoranda of the same is at hand. During that service I endeavoured to keep as correct as possible a daily journal of events, and from that journal I have prepared this brief history of the company, and I trust that my comrades who may read this will excuse any inaccuracies that in their opinion may appear; for it is my desire to place before you a correct history of Company F, the first company of volunteers that left Newport on the 17th of April, 1861, for the defence of the Stars and Stripes in the great war of the rebellion.

Charles H. Clarke.

CHAPTER 1

Call To Arms

Early in the month of April, 1861, several of the Southern States having withdrawn from the Union, forts, arsenals and navy yards within the limits of those States were taken possession of by the Confederate forces. On the 12th of April, Fort Sumter, at Charleston, S. C., was fired upon, and after two days' bombardment by the rebels, commanded by General Beauregard, the garrison, comprising seventy United States Regulars, commanded by Major Robert Anderson, surrendered the fort. Meanwhile the National Capital at Washington was in danger, and on the 15th of April Abraham Lincoln issued his proclamation, calling for seventy-five thousand troops for the defence of the city of Washington.

Governor Sprague, of Rhode Island, tendered the services of one regiment of Infantry, and one battery of Light Artillery, which being accepted by the Secretary of War, the Governor at once sent a telegram to Colonel George W. Tew, commanding the Newport Artillery company, asking how many men of his command would go to Washington for the defence of the Capital. Colonel Tew replied that he would go, with fifty men. April 16th, Colonel Tew received another telegram from the Governor, directing him to recruit his company to one hundred, and to report at Providence, armed and equipped, upon receipt of orders. At that time the Newport Artillery were as well equipped as any company in the State.

They were armed with the latest improved Springfield rifles. They had just purchased, at their own expense, fifty artillery sabres of the latest French pattern. They had likewise, the year preceding, had made to their order new military overcoats, which no other company in the State was at that time provided with. These overcoats and sabres were afterwards purchased of them by the State of Rhode Island, and were used for equipping the 1st Battery.

On April 16th Colonel Tew called a meeting of the company, and after reading the telegrams received from the Governor that day, made a patriotic speech, and was followed by Mayor Cranston, who was present. Colonel Tew then requested those of the company that would volunteer to go to Washington, to step to the front, when thirty-three of the thirty-nine active members of the company responded. A call was then made for volunteers to fill up the company to the required number of one hundred men, and in a very short time there were more men applied than could be taken.

That evening the company paraded through the streets of the city, to the inspiriting music of a fife and drum, and were dismissed at 10 p.m., to meet again on the receipt of orders from Providence, to be announced by the discharge of three guns on the Mall, and by the ringing of the church bells.

At 7 a.m., Wednesday, April 17th, a mounted courier arrived from Providence with orders for Colonel Tew to report that day in Providence with his company. Colonel Tew, upon the receipt of the order, sent word by return courier that he would be in Providence with his company at 2 p.m.

At 8 a.m., one of the company's brass guns was dragged by hand to the Mall and fired three times by the gun squad that had remained in the armory all night so as to be on hand when orders came.

Never before in the known history of the city was there so much excitement as was caused by the firing of those guns. Business of all kinds was suspended for the time being, and the people began to realize that the time had come for action.

When the orders came that morning, Colonel George W. Tew was at work at his trade, a mason, on Wellington Avenue. On receiving the order he laid down his trowel and other tools, adopted the trade of a soldier, and for four long years he served his country with credit to himself and to the State of Rhode Island.

First Sergeant A. P. Sherman was driving on his market wagon attending to his morning trade when he heard the signal guns. Leaving his team on the street, he started at once for the armoury on Clarke street, and commenced to form the company.

In less than one hour the company were in line and ready to start. Like the minute men of Revolutionary times, they left their bench, their desks, and farm, at the call to arms. Thames street, Washington Square and Clarke Street were thronged with people. The artillery was at that time as at present the pride of Newport and it is not strange that so much interest was manifested, and, besides, they were about to leave home and friends, not knowing whether they would ever return. They went from pure patriotism and love of the Old Flag; and it is an undisputed fact today that had it not been for the promptitude with which the first troops responded to the call of the President, the city of Washington would have been taken by the rebel forces.

At the armoury there were there assembled many prominent citizens, Mayor W. H. Cranston and several of the clergy. Speech making and hand shaking were indulged in for some time, and at 11.30 a.m. the company marched to Sayer's Wharf by way of Clarke, Touro and Thames streets, escorted by about fifty past members of the company. On the wharf, Rev. Samuel Adlam, of the First Baptist Church, offered prayer, and was followed by Mayor Cranston and Hon. Charles C. Van Zandt, in brief addresses. Rev. Thatcher Thayer, who had for many years been chaplain of the Artillery company, and still holds that position, (1891) offered a touching prayer in behalf of the company and the cause for the support and defence of which they were now about to leave home, kindred and friends, after which the benediction was pronounced by Rev. Henry Jackson, D. D. A brief season was then allowed for individual leave-takings, and at 1 p.m. the company marched on board steamer Perry for Providence to form a part of Rhode Island's first regiment in the war of the rebellion.

Following is a correct roll of the company, as copied from the muster-out roll of the regiment:

Company Roster

Captain,—	George W. Tew.
1st Lieutenant,—	William A. Steadman.
2nd "	Benjamin L. Slocum.
Ensign—,	James H. Chappell.
1st Sergeant, —	Augustus P. Sherman.
2nd "	Thomas S. Burdick.
3rd "	John S. Coggeshall.
4th "	Edward S. Hammond.
1st Corporal,—	John D. Washburne.
2nd "	Benedict F. Smith.
3rd "	Ray B. Tayer.
4th "	Henry L. Nicolai.

Privates.

15

John A. Abbott.
Albert N. Burdick.
John H. Bacheller.
Charles Barker, Jr.
William Booth.
Jeremiah Brown.
Thomas Brownell.
Benjamin D. Carlisle.
Allen Caswell.
Edward F. Clarke.
Gustavus A. Clarke.
David M. Coggeshall, Jr.
Robert D. Coggeshall.
Perry B. Dawley.
William P. Denman.
Silas D. DeBlois.
William H. Durfee.
Benjamin Easton, Jr.
William J. Eldridge.
John Fludder.
Thomas J. Harrington.
Rowland R. Hazard.
Samuel Hilton.
George A. Hudson.
William Keating.
Theodore W. King.
Israel F. Lake, Jr.
Henry B. Landers.
Overton G. Langley.
George P. Lawton.
David Little.
John B. Mason.
Daniel A. McCann.
Walden H. Mason.
George H. Palmer.
Edwin H. Peabody.
Peyton H. Randolph.
Benjamin H. Rogers.
John F. Scott.
Thomas Sharpe.

Charles B. Barlow.
George C. Almy.
Christopher E. Barker.
Andrew P. Bashford.
Daniel Boss.
Adelbert P. Bryant.
Henry Bull, Jr.
Robert Carlisle.
Charles H. Clarke.
Frederic A. Clarke.
Joshua P. Clarke.
Lawton Coggeshall.
Robert Crane.
Benjamin F. Davis.
Lance DeJongh.
Stephen DeBlois.
Henry T. Easton.
John F. Easton.
Edmund W. Fales.
Augustus French.
Joseph J. Gould.
William Hamilton.
Benjamin C. Hubbard.
Harris Keables.
Edwin A. Kelley.
William H. King.
Thomas O. Lake.
John B. Landers.
Charles E. Lawton.
Thomas H. Lawton.
Charles L. Littlefield.
James Markham.
William M. Minkler.
Michael A. Nolan.
Frederic J. Peabody.
John P. Peckham.
John Rogers.
John H. Robinson.
Thomas Scott.
Bartlett L. Simmons.

John B. F. Smith.
Charles Southwick.
George W. Taber.
William H. Thayer.
Arthur R. Tuell.
William H. Waldron.
Charles S. Weaver.
Edward Wilson.

George B. Smith.
John Stark.
Edward Terrell.
William Towle.
James P. Vose.
George S. Ward.
George R. White.
William H. Young.

To be added to this roll, should be the names of James H. Taylor, John S. Engs, and James W. Lyon, members of the regimental non-commissioned staff, who were members of the company from Newport, but their names do not appear on the muster-out roll of the company.

On arriving at Providence, the company marched to Railroad Hall, on Exchange Place, where they were to be quartered until such time as the regiment could be uniformed and equipped. The organization of the regiment commenced at once. Ambrose E. Burnside was appointed colonel; Joseph S. Pitman, lieutenant colonel; John S. Slocum, 1st major; Joseph P. Balch, 2nd major; Charles H. Merriman, adjutant; Rev. Augustus Woodbury, chaplain. All company officers were elected by the company, approved and commissioned by the Governor. The position in line of the companies and the letter by which they were to be known, was drawn by lot by the captains. The Newport company was designated by the letter F, and drew third position in line, which constituted them the colour company of the regiment. In the making up of the non-commissioned staff, there were appointed James H. Taylor as hospital steward, James W. Lyon as ordnance sergeant, and John S. Engs as sergeant major; Edward S. Hammond was appointed as left general guide of the regiment.

As fast as the uniforms could be made, they were issued to the companies. These consisted of a light blue blouse, of the Garibaldi pattern, dark grey pants, and Kossuth hat, with the brim turned up on the right side, and fastened to the crown with a brass plate, eagle shaped. Instead of overcoats, we were provided with red woollen blankets, with a slit in the centre, to wear over our shoulders in bad weather; also one grey blanket, knapsack, to contain our extra clothing, haversack, canteen, tin plate, knife and fork, spoon, and tin cup.

17

CHAPTER 2

Off For the Front

On Saturday, April 19th, the first detachment, made up of details from all the companies, to the number of nearly six hundred men, including the regimental band, of twenty-four men, were in readiness to start for Washington. The regiment formed on Exchange Place at noon, where they received a costly and beautiful regimental flag, of silk, presented by the ladies of Providence. Colonel Burnside, on receiving the precious gift, remarked as follows:—

> I know that the gallant men I carry away will prove themselves worthy of the beautiful banner presented to them by you. We are fully impressed with the fact that we take with us your most fervent prayers, and we shall constantly feel that your eyes are upon us. God grant that we may yet see the Union out of danger. Bidding you an affectionate farewell, and thanking you in behalf of my command, for your kindness, I feel that I can assure you in the name of each and every one of them, that no act of theirs shall ever cause you to regret this your generous and patriotic contribution to the cause we mutually cherish.

The flag was then given in charge of Company F, the colour company of the regiment, Charles Becherer, of Company G, being detailed as colour sergeant.

A short regimental parade was made through the streets of Providence to the wharf where steamer *Empire State* was lying with steam up, in readiness to take the regiment to New York. At about 2.30 p.m. the boat cast off her lines and steamed down the bay and through the harbour of Newport out to sea. When the steamer was passing Long Wharf, a salute was fired by a gun squad of the past members of the Newport Artillery. A salute was also fired from Fort Adams, as the steamer passed on her way out to sea.

Sunday morning, April 20th, arrived in New York. The regiment, with its baggage, was at once transferred to the United States Government transport *Coatzacolcos*, on board of which we remained all that day, and Monday steamed away for Annapolis.

A tug boat which spoke to us in the afternoon, gave us the information that the Norfolk navy yard had been blown up and destroyed by orders from our government. At daylight the next morning we came in sight of Fortress Monroe, and sailing on up Chesapeake Bay, anchored for the night, and the next day steamed up into the harbour of Annapolis and landed. We were kindly received by the officers of the United States Naval Academy, who furnished us with quarters in the government building for the night.

General Benjamin F. Butler, of Massachusetts, was there in command of the United States forces, composed mostly of New England troops.

Thursday morning we set out on the road to Annapolis Junction. We were told by inhabitants we met that we never would reach Washington, as the road was in the possession of Confederate troops and their friends; but we tramped along, and overtook the 71st New York Regiment at noon, halting an hour or two in their company, and after having had a good rest, about 4 o'clock resumed our march for the Junction, discovering no signs of the enemy as we proceeded, and at about 8 p.m. halted for the night.

We encamped in a field beside the railroad, posting sentinels on all sides, as we expected an attack at this place. Camp fires were kindled, supper prepared and eaten, after which preparations were made for the night. The 71st New York coming up and halting at our bivouac, we exchanged greetings with them, furnished them with hot coffee, and informed them, as they took their departure on the road, that it was a short march for them to the Junction—"only nine more miles." A member of the 71st afterwards composed a song entitled "Nine Miles to the Junction," the words of which were as follows:

The troops of Rhode Island were posted along
On the road from Annapolis station,
As the 71st Regiment, one thousand strong,
Went on in defence of the nation:
We'd been marching all day, in the sun's scorching rays,
With two biscuits a day as our rations,
When we asked Governor Sprague to show us the way,

And "How many miles to the Junction?"
[Repeat:]

The Rhode Island boys cheered us on out of sight,
After giving the following injunction:
"Just to keep up your courage—you'll get there tonight,
For 'it's only nine miles to the Junction!'"
They gave us hot coffee, a grasp of the hand,
Which cheered and refreshed our exhaustion;
We reached in six hours the long promised land,
For 'twas "only nine miles to the Junction."

And now as we meet them in Washington's streets,
They always salute us with unction;
And still the old cry someone will repeat—
"It's only nine miles to the Junction!"
Three cheers for the warm hearted Rhode Island boys,
May each be true to his function;
And whene'er we meet, let us each other greet,
With "Only nine miles to the Junction."

Nine cheers for the flag under which we will fight,
If the traitors should dare to assail it.
One cheer for each mile that we made on that night,
When 'twas "Only nine miles to the Junction."
With hearts thus united, our breasts to the foe—
Once more with delight will we hail it;
If duty should call us, still onward we'll go,
If even "nine miles to the Junction."

This was set to the air, "Tother side o' Jordan," and was adopted into the regiment, becoming one of our camp fire songs.

During the night, after the departure of the 71st, nothing transpired to disturb us.

At about 4 o'clock a.m. April 26th, we were once more on the road to the Junction, which we reached at about 5.30 a.m., and at once commenced loading baggage and provisions on the cars. At 9 a.m., everything being in readiness and the road reported clear, we started for Washington, where we arrived about noon, and were at once marched to the Patent Office, on 7th street, where we were to be quartered until a site for a camp could be selected.

Tuesday, April 30th, the second detachment of the regiment arrived, in command of Lieutenant Colonel Pitman, and on May 1st the regiment was paraded in front of the Patent Office, the occasion being the raising of the Stars and Stripes on that building. The flag was hoisted by President Lincoln, after which the regiment was drilled by Colonel Burnside, under review by the President and members of the Cabinet.

Thursday, May 2nd, the Light Battery arrived from Providence, in command of Captain Charles H. Tompkins, and in the afternoon the entire regiment marched to the Capitol grounds, and was sworn into the United States service, by Major McDowell, of the Regular army.

CHAPTER 3

Life in Camp

Preparations were at once made to go into camp. A detail of mechanics was made from the regiment, and under the direction of Lieutenant Walker, of Company E, the requisite buildings were erected, and on May 10th the regiment went into camp in their new quarters, on the Keating farm, near the Bladensburg road, about a mile north of the Capitol. It was named Camp Sprague, in honour of Rhode Island's Governor.

Ten rows of buildings had been constructed, parallel with each other, for company quarters, a row for each company, with a street about fifteen feet in width between the buildings. The quarters of each company comprised six squad rooms, each room having accommodations for a non-commissioned officer and eighteen men, and on three sides of each sleeping room were bunks; there was also an outer room, or porch, with a table extending lengthwise, for use as a dining room. The company officers occupied a building separated from the men by a narrow street. The regimental officers and band were very pleasantly located in a shady grove, in cottage shaped buildings, with *piazza* in front, standing in the rear of and at right angles with the company quarters.

We soon got settled in our new home at Camp Sprague, and commenced at once the duties of soldier life. Previous to this we had been in an unsettled condition, taking our meals at restaurants and using the Patent Office for sleeping quarters, with not much duty to perform, except answering to roll-calls. Now, however, we knew just what was expected of us every day. Our duties commenced soon after daylight, ending at 9 p.m. At about 5 a.m. we were aroused from our slumbers by the beating of the reveille, which duty was performed by Drum Major Ben. West and his fife and drum band, when each man was required to turn out, take his place in line in the company street, and answer to his name. This duty was performed with a great deal of promptitude, at first, but after a while some of the boys did not get started out of their bunks in time to complete their toilet, and often would appear in line thinly clad, and it was no unusual thing to see some appear bareheaded and without shoes or stockings.

One squad of the company was particularly noted for their tardiness at reveille. I don't think this was owing to any neglect on the part of the sergeant in charge; for Sergeant Hammond was wont to boast that he had "the banner squad," and he exacted of them everything in the line of duty. But two of his men appeared to be impressed with the notion that the nights in that latitude were too short to satisfy their demands for sleep. They would lie in bed and wait until the last roll of the drum, then tumbling out, they would have hardly sufficient time to take their places in line to answer to their names when called.

One morning, during roll-call, the company were surprised to see running from the direction of Sergeant Hammond's quarters two men to all appearances of African descent. The First Sergeant, not knowing who they were, ordered them to stand aside, and then continued the calling of the roll. When the names of John B. M. and L. DeJ. were called, two "coloured gentlemen" responded. The first sergeant, after roll-call, reprimanded them for appearing in such condition, advising them to in future be more prompt at roll-call. Some one or more merciless wags among their comrades had, during the silent watches of the night, and while they slept the sleep of the just, surreptitiously decorated their countenances with burnt cork. Of course Hammond knew nothing of it until their appearance at roll-call; but I do not think that afterwards there were any of Hammond's squad tardy at roll-call.

Directly after reveille came the sick-call, when those who required medical attention went to the hospital; breakfast at 7, guard-mount at 8 a.m., company drills and target practise from 9 to 11 a.m., dinner at noon. In the afternoon, battalion drill of the entire regiment, and at sunset dress parade, which on pleasant days was witnessed by a large number of the citizens and notables of Washington, including President Lincoln and members of the Cabinet. After the parade, the regiment formed in double column, closed *en masse,* when our chaplain, Rev. Augustus Woodbury, read a portion of scripture, followed by prayer, the service closing with singing the doxology by the entire regiment, accompanied by the band, with most solemn and impressive effect; tattoo roll-call at 9 p.m., taps at 9.30, when lights were extinguished and every man was supposed to be in his bunk for the night; but on many occasions there was more of supposition than reality.

Notwithstanding the circumstance that we were United States soldiers, and as such bound to obey the army regulations, there were in nearly every squad men who would at times commit acts that had they realized the consequences if found out, they would not have suffered themselves to do. To take men from civil life, with no previous military training, and subject them to army discipline, is a difficult task to accomplish, and is a work of time; nor is it a matter for wonder that men forget their being soldiers and liable to severe punishment for misdemeanours.

After taps, it was the custom of the officer of the day to make the rounds of the camp to make sure that all lights were out and everything quiet in the company quarters. Sometimes this officer, if he manifested a disposition to be officious in the discharge of his duties, came to grief. There was one who, when detailed as officer of the day, generally had about all the business he cared to attend to, in the vicinity of Company F quarters, after taps. A candle would be left burning on the table in a room, to attract the officer's attention, who on seeing it would shout at the top of his voice, "Put out that light in Company F quarters!"

Someone in bed would reply, "Go to H—ades, you old granny!"

The officer, entering, would be deluged with a shower of tin pans and plates, placed on a shelf purposely rigged directly over the entrance, propped up by sticks, and at the proper time tripped by means of a string manipulated by some person to the officer unknown, the light being at the same instant extinguished by someone in the plot, the transaction overwhelming the officer with impotent wrath.

May 21st, John Abbott and Thomas H. Lawton were discharged from the company on account of disability, returning home.

May 23rd, Governor Sprague left camp for home, to be inaugurated as Governor for another year. A detail of thirty men from the regiment was made today, and placed under command of Lieutenant Tower, of Company E, to operate a ferry for transporting troops across the river to Alexandria. They worked only nights, returning to camp at daylight in the morning. Company F furnished five men—Sergeant Burdick, John B. F. Smith, Andrew P. Bashford, George R. White, and Peyton Randolph, all of whom had been sailors previous to enlistment in the army, and consequently were familiar with that line of duty, and to them it was mere pastime.

24

Although away from home and friends, we as sons of old Newport could not permit 'Lection day to pass without notice. Nearly all of us had sent us from home boxes containing cake and blue eggs, and with these as a basis, we made preparations to celebrate the day. At sunrise we flung to the breeze a beautiful American flag, from the 1st sergeant's quarters. This flag, presented to us by Mr. William Vernon, of Newport, is still in the possession of the Newport Artillery company. A salute was fired by our battery, in honour of the day, and at 9 a.m. a table was spread in the quarters, with plenty of cake and egg pop. Private George C. Almy was deputed to call on and invite the company and regimental officers to visit us and partake of the good things. It was a very enjoyable occasion, Colonel Burnside and Chaplain Woodbury making some pleasant remarks.

May 31st, David Little, Fred J. Peabody and William Waldron, of Company F, were discharged on surgeon's certificate, for disability, and returned home.

About the first of June there were rumours in camp of a movement of troops; extra rations were cooked, and other preparations made for a forward movement.

June 6th, John S. Engs, who had been company clerk, was promoted to the position of sergeant-major of the regiment, to fill the vacancy caused by the resignation of John P. Shaw, who had been promoted to lieutenant in the 2nd Rhode Island Regiment, and Augustus French was appointed company clerk.

CHAPTER 4

Expedition to Harper's Ferry

On Saturday, 8th of June, orders came for an expedition to Harper's Ferry. The day before starting, we had issued to us new caps of the French forage pattern, also white linen havelocks, to wear over them, which added greatly to the appearance of the men, being likewise a decided protection from the scorching rays of the June sun.

June 10th, the regiment broke camp, and marching to Washington took cars for Baltimore, arriving at which place we marched across the city to embark for Chambersburg, Pennsylvania. We had anticipated trouble in marching through the streets of Baltimore; but the roughs of the then rebellious city knew better than to oppose the passage of a regiment and battery armed and equipped as was the 1st Rhode Island. The regiment marched across the city from the depot where we landed, without a halt, with its band playing national airs. We were well supplied with ammunition, and the battery could have swept the streets of any mob essaying to obstruct its progress. We soon reached and boarded the cars, arriving at Chambersburg at noon, 11th, and starting again by rail for Greencastle, Pennsylvania, which place we reached at sunset the same day.

After leaving the train we marched about three miles beyond the town, where we bivouacked for the night in a grove beside the road. We had no tents nor rations, the wagons not having come up. The regiment formed in a hollow square, stacked their muskets, and lay down on the ground, without covering, other than their blankets; sentinels were posted on the road, the battery parked in the rear of the regiment, and every precaution taken against surprise during the night. Tents arrived the next morning at daylight, but no rations. The tents we pitched and made preparations for a few days' stay. Troops were all the time coming and marching. The army to which we were at that time attached, comprised about nine thousand men, commanded by General Patterson, and was organizing for an attack upon Harper's Ferry.

June 12th, at noon, Governor Sprague rejoined us, having left Rhode Island at once on learning that we had departed from Washington.

At about sunset, while many of the regiment were seated on fences watching the passing troops, a Pennsylvania regiment came along the road, halting a few moments for rest in front of our camp. Directly some of our regiment discovered a man in one of the Pennsylvania companies who had been arrested by our regiment as a spy, while we were quartered at the Patent office in Washington. A rush was made for him, he was dragged from his company, and but for the intervention of some of our officers he would have been strung up on the spot.

Saturday morning, June 13th, we once more started, our destination being Williamsport, Maryland, distant fourteen miles. This was one of the hardest marches that we made. The weather was hot, the roads rough and dusty, and when we went into camp at Williamsport, there was only one officer and fourteen men of our company with the colours, present. The balance of the company were exhausted, and were straggling along the road, but by sunset they had all arrived in camp. We pitched our tents in the woods and rested the whole of Sunday.

Monday morning, June 15th, broke camp at daylight, and started on the road for Harper's Ferry. We had barely got started, when a mounted orderly arrived from Hagerstown, Maryland, with orders for Colonel Burnside to return with his regiment and battery to Washington, at once. Harper's Ferry had been evacuated by the rebels, who were also moving in the direction of Washington. Our regiment and battery set out at once on the road for Hagerstown, arriving there at noon. Without stopping we marched on through Funkstown, arriving at Boonsboro, Maryland, at 3 p.m., where we halted for a rest.

We found the people of the place loyal, and disposed to show us every possible attention. We halted on the public square, or common, and the ladies of the town gathered in large numbers and supplied many of us with cake and other refreshments. Here the regiment and battery rested until 5 p.m., when the march was resumed. Entering a pass of the South Mountain, the acclivity looming up on both sides, every precaution was taken against any possible surprise by the enemy.

27

The battery was divided, one-half in the advance and the remainder in the rear of the column.

At 9 p.m. we reached Middletown, where the people showed themselves in large numbers, as we passed their quiet homes. We made no stop at Middletown, but tramped along, tired and hungry, stopping about midnight and camping on a hill on the outskirts of Frederick City, Maryland, having marched thirty-six miles since daylight. Men from all the companies soon collected rails and built a camp-fire, illuminating the surrounding country and causing the ringing of a fire alarm in Frederick City.

At 4 a.m. June 18th, we broke camp and marched into Frederick, halting at some old barracks, said to have been built during the Revolutionary war. We were the first Union troops that had entered Frederick City since the commencement of hostilities, and the event naturally caused no little stir among the inhabitants of that semi-rebellious city. Nearly if not quite all its prominent citizens were in sympathy with the rebel cause, and we were consequently not regarded by them with any degree of favour. The presence, however, of twelve hundred well drilled and disciplined troops and a battery of six rifled guns, proved a quite potent reminder of what might be expected should there be any undue interference. Soon after entering Frederick, our company was marched to a restaurant and provided with an excellent breakfast, after which we returned to the old barracks.

We were given permission by our officers to look about the city, with orders to report in camp at noon. Many of the citizens were found to be true Union men, by whom we were courteously received and kindly treated, and I don't believe that during our brief stay in town any member of the regiment, either by word or deed, left any unfavourable impression among the inhabitants. In the afternoon, just previous to the departure of the regiment, a deputation of Union citizens, both men and women, waited upon us and presented to Mrs. Kady Brownell an elegant American flag. Mrs. Brownell was the wife of Robert S. Brownell, of Company H, and when her husband enlisted, in Providence, she insisted on accompanying him, and was with the regiment during its entire term of service, in all its long marches sharing its privations and enduring its hardships.

At the battle of Bull Run she was on the skirmish line with her husband, who was at the time a sergeant. She wore a uniform somewhat similar to that of the regiment, and was proficient in the use of a revolver and a short, straight sword, that she always wore suspended at her side.

At about 4 p.m., the regiment took up the line of march for the depot, to take cars for Washington. In marching through one of the principal streets leading to the depot, a crowd of rebel toughs issued from a side street, and following us, volunteered insulting remarks concerning us and the flag. Captain Tew, of our company, had at that time a coloured servant, who had been with us for some time. This sooty individual, who was known by the name of John, had somewhere on the march picked up an antiquated sword and belt, which he had buckled on and felt very proud of. The sight of this negro, thus attired, appeared to kindle the wrath of Frederick City's chivalry to such an extent that they attempted to seize and make way with the boy, and for a short time the excitement ran high. The colour sergeant, seeing that an attack upon us was threatened, drew his revolver and stood on the defensive.

The right wing of the regiment, not being aware of the disturbance, continued on its march. Lieutenant Colonel Pitman, who was in command of the left wing, noticing the aspect of things, took prompt action, halting the companies, most of the men of F company loading their muskets, as they expected that the mob, which by this time had largely increased in numbers, would make an attack. At this juncture Colonel Burnside rode up and was about to issue some order to our officers, when a squad of city police, or home guard, appeared upon the scene and dispersed the mob, after which we resumed our march, soon arriving at the depot, where we took a train for Washington, reaching that place at daylight the next morning, June 19th.

Company F was immediately detailed to unload tents and other baggage from the cars. The regiment marched at once to our old quarters at Camp Sprague. While engaged on our work of unloading, our ever thoughtful commissary sent us a barrel of Camp Sprague ginger-bread, for lunch, and some good friend of the company, I never knew who, furnished us with a barrel of "conversation water" to wash it down with. We finished our work at 5 a.m., and marched out to camp, where we found a nice breakfast awaiting us. We resumed camp duties at once. Although we had been on a ten days' tramp, and had made one of the longest marches that had up to that time been made, in one day, by any troops, and had not during the whole time been over-stocked with rations, all the boys were in good condition and in readiness for any duty required of them.

Saturday June 22nd, at 3 a.m., the camp was aroused by the beating of drums, and for a few minutes all was excitement, until it was announced that the occasion of the alarm was the arrival at our camp of the 2nd Rhode Island regiment, *via* Washington, which place they had reached a few hours previous, and were waiting outside to allow us time to form our regiment so as to receive them in true military style, which was done a few minutes later, and K Company, Captain Charles W. Turner, our company asked to breakfast with us that morning. The 2nd Regiment went into camp in tents in a shady grove adjoining us, and as long as we remained in Washington, both regiments mounted guard and had dress parade together every day.

Many officers of the Second had seen service in our regiment previous to the formation of theirs, and we were intimately acquainted with many of its men, particularly those from Newport; and the men of our company will always look back with a great deal of pleasure to those days in the summer of '61, when the men of the two regiments passed so many pleasant hours in each others' society. The associations formed at that time, and later on in the war, between soldiers, were fraternal in their character, and to this day the same feeling exists among members of the Grand Army of the Republic, and will continue as long as the men that were associated with us shall live.

June 28th, the 1st and 2nd Regiments, with the band of each, and the two Rhode Island light batteries, made a parade in the city of Washington, marching up through Pennsylvania Avenue to the White House, and counter-marching and passing in review before the President and other notables, among whom was the venerable General Winfield Scott, then so aged and feeble as to be unable to stand, sitting in a chair as the troops moved past. The parade was a grand showing for Little Rhody, over two thousand men in line, and so finely officered, armed and equipped. The Washington papers were enthusiastic in their praises of our soldierly appearance. In this parade we marched full company front, three ranks deep. The Hardee tactics were then in use in the army, but on this occasion we observed the three-rank formation prescribed in the Scott tactics previous to the war.

The old general was highly pleased to see troops thus formed, as he was the originator of the three-rank formation, and I do not think he ever before or after saw so many troops arranged in that manner. We returned to camp at 5 p.m., and at evening parade Colonel Burnside complimented the troops highly for their soldierly bearing and general behaviour while in the city that day.

Soon after the arrival of the 2nd Regiment, a change was made in the detail for camp guard. Previous to this there were ten men and a non-commissioned officer detailed every day from each company, for guard duty. But owing to the increased size of the camp, it was necessary that more men should be detailed, consequently an order was issued that a full company from each regiment be detailed every day for that duty. This new order of things was the occasion for considerable argument among the members of Company F, and we had men with us who were always ready for an argument, particularly if they believed they would be benefited by it. Albeit, while most of the company were ever ready and willing to obey every order emanating from proper authority, there were yet some who always reserved the right, as they thought, to growl.

Some contended that it was contrary to army regulations, and that Company F could not be thus detailed, they were the colour company of the regiment, and in case of an alarm, if the entire company were detailed for extraneous duty the colours would be without a guard. The matter was finally referred to Colonel Burnside, who at once decided that the colour guard of eight men were exempt from general guard duty, but the balance of the company would mount guard. It would seem as though this should have settled the matter, but such was not the fact; in a few days Company F was detailed for guard duty, and at the proper time we were marched upon the parade ground, the customary evolutions pertaining to guard mount gone through with, and the order was given to march the guard off to the guard-house. Off we started, the band playing, but on our arrival at the guard-house our first sergeant was not with us, and on looking in the direction of the parade ground he was observed standing there alone, Robinson Crusoe like, "monarch of all he surveyed."

On being requested by the adjutant to report for duty, he objected to doing so, and went to his quarters. He was soon ordered to report at headquarters, charged with disobedience of orders, but was allowed to give his reasons for not complying with orders relating to guard duty, which he readily did. They were that a 1st sergeant of a company was not a duty sergeant, and was consequently by the regulations exempt from such duty while in camp. The matter being referred to Colonel Burnside, that officer promptly ruled that the sergeant was right, and ever after the 1st sergeants of companies were relieved from service in that direction while in camp.

It was a notable circumstance, which I wish to record here, that while Colonel Burnside always exacted of us a strict compliance with all orders, he was at the same time ready and willing to listen and act upon any complaint from officers or men, and invariably his decisions were just. He treated all alike, and was ever on the lookout for the welfare and comfort of the men. As an illustration of General Burnside's ideas of duty, it was decided to erect a temporary structure for the purpose of holding religious services on the Sabbath. One day the sergeant-major made application to the captains of companies for a detail of mechanics for this work, in response to which details were sent from all except one of the companies, the captain of this company stating to the sergeant-major in response that he had no mechanics, his company being composed wholly of business men and clerks.

This circumstance being duly reported to Colonel Burnside, he instructed the sergeant major to direct the captain of that company to detail ten men at once, as there were some foundation holes to dig, and he did not wish mechanics to do that sort of work.

Fourth of July was celebrated by both regiments in camp. There was a review of the regiments and batteries, and services held appropriate to the day, in which were included singing, music by the bands, and an oration by Rev. Father Quinn. In the afternoon we had sports of all kinds; a member of the second regiment gave a tight rope performance, and a member of the battery procured and turned loose a pig, well greased, said porker to become the property of the one that could catch and hold him; prizes were offered for the champion wrestler and clog dancer, respectively, both of which were captured by members of Company F, notwithstanding they had to compete with picked men from both regiments. James Markham took the clog dancer prize, and John H. Robinson laid every man on his back that presented himself before him.

We now commenced to have early morning drill. Every morning, directly after sick call, all the companies of the regiment moved out of camp in different directions, for one hour's drill before breakfast. This new order was not relished any better by the officers than the men, there was seldom more than one officer with us on these occasions, and often, as soon as a point outside the camp had been reached, the order to rest was given, particularly if there was a shady place handy; and I am of the opinion that those morning drills did not add much to our efficiency as soldiers.

On the morning of July 9th, the battery of the 2nd Regiment were marching out for drill, and when a short distance from camp one of the ammunition chests exploded, killing one man, and mortally wounding the corporal of the gun, the latter dying in a few hours; the caisson was blown to pieces, and the wheel horses fatally injured. That afternoon funeral services were held in the camp of the 2nd Regiment, and the remains of the deceased comrades were that evening put on board the cars for transportation to Providence.

About the 10th of July, there were rumours in camp of an intended advance into Virginia; extra rations were ordered, and new shoes issued to the company.

July 11th. Edward Wilson, of F company, who had deserted at Frederick City, returned to camp, was placed in the guard house, and at dress parade, July 12th, his dishonourable discharge was read to the regiment. William H. Durfee and George S. Ward were the same day discharged on account of disability.

July 14th. We received orders to be in readiness to march at short notice, in light marching order, with no tents or unnecessary baggage. The order was received by the men, generally, with much enthusiasm, and as a decided relief from the monotonous existence incident to camp duty. The men had come out there to assist in putting down the rebellion and sustaining the honour of the flag, and as their term of service drew towards a close, they felt anxious that their journey to and sojourn in Washington and vicinity should be productive in results.

CHAPTER 5

Advance into Virginia, and Battle of Bull Run

On the morning of July 16th, came the order to move. F Company mounted guard, that morning, in marching order, with forty rounds of ammunition in our boxes, three days' rations in our haversacks, and blankets strapped on our backs. Both regiments formed on the parade ground at 10 a.m. Our company was relieved from guard and took its position in line, with the colours.

Both regiments marched into Washington, the battery of the 2nd Regiment accompanying us. The camp was left in charge of about sixty men of the regiment, who had been on the sick roll, but had so far recovered as to be in condition for camp duty. Corporal Nicolai and Private Terrell, of our company, had been on the sick roll, but insisted on taking their place in the ranks, and marched into the city, but were obliged to return to camp the same night, not being sufficiently strong to endure the march.

Arrived in the city, we halted on Pennsylvania Avenue, waiting for the other regiments of our brigade, comprising, besides our own and the 2nd, the 7th New York and 2nd New Hampshire and 2nd Rhode Island Light Battery, to join us, the whole comprising the Second Brigade, Second Division, commanded by General Hunter. It was late in the afternoon before we were ordered to move. All day troops had been crossing Long Bridge, and we had to wait until the whole of the First Division of infantry, artillery and cavalry had crossed. The army consisted of about forty-four thousand men, commanded by General McDowell; there was also attached to the column a battalion of United States Marines.

Our brigade crossed Long Bridge at about 4 p.m., and marched

34

with our entire Division as far as Anandale, where we bivouacked for the night in the fields beside the road. Soon after halting, the boys began to think about supper, and little fires were kindled, coffee made, in our tin cups, and it is my opinion that the greater part of the three days' rations issued to us that morning were consumed that night. After supper, rolling our blankets about us, we lay down on the ground and enjoyed a good night's rest, notwithstanding that quite a shower of rain fell during the night.

We were on the road again soon after daylight the next morning. Hunter's Division, to which we were attached, marched on the direct road to Fairfax Court House. Soon after leaving Anandale, signs of the enemy's presence began to be visible: the roads were blocked with trees that had been felled and piled across the way, some of the obstructions so completely filling the road, that we were obliged to make a detour around them, through the fields. A company of sappers and miners attached to the 71st New York, and a detail of men from the 2nd New Hampshire, with their axes cleared the road for the artillery to pass. Earthworks were occasionally found in the rear of these obstructions, thrown across the road; but in every instance they had been abandoned as we approached them; in some of these there were evidences of their having been occupied by the rebels the night previous.

The 2nd Rhode Island, which was at the head of the column, was now ordered to send out skirmishers; also the carbineer company, Captain Goddard, of our regiment, was detailed for skirmish duty. We advanced cautiously, and soon a halt was ordered. Firing at the front was heard, where our skirmishers were driving the rebels back. Colonel Burnside, riding through our ranks, ordered us to load our muskets and be sure and obey all orders from our officers.

It was now about 9 a.m., and we knew that we were nearing Fairfax Court House, and knew also that the enemy were there in force and would resist our advance, which they no doubt would have done, had it not been that they had knowledge of the other two Divisions of our army under Generals Tyler and Heintzelman, who were advancing rapidly on other roads leading to Fairfax.

After a halt of about fifteen minutes, the order to advance was given, and in a short time we marched into Fairfax Court House without having fired a gun, the rebels having retreated in such haste as to leave their tents standing, and in many of their camps we found clothing and baggage of various kinds. The 2nd Rhode Island Regiment pursued the retreating enemy a short distance beyond the town. As we marched into the place the band played Yankee Doodle, and the colour sergeant of the 2nd New Hampshire mounted to the cupola and hoisted his flag.

We soon had possession of the town, and the regiments of the division were stationed in different localities. We captured a Southern mail that had just arrived, and soon the ground in the vicinity of the Post Office was covered with mail matter of all kinds. We had quite a treat reading some of the letters that were picked up, particularly those written by fair rebels in the sunny south, who never dreamed that eyes other than those of their adored would scan their contents; but in time of war things are "mighty onsartin," to which love letters constitute no exception.

Nearly all the inhabitants had left the place on our approach, leaving behind their household furniture and goods. About all the residences of the so called chivalry were left in charge of one or more coloured servants of the family, and in some instances these houses were protected from plunder through a guard placed over them by order of our commanding officer, while many of the homes of the poorer classes were broken into and plundered of articles of all kinds. For the first three hours of our occupation of the place, this state of affairs existed. The men, not being restrained of their liberty, roamed wherever they saw fit, and everybody, officers as well as men, appeared anxious to gobble up everything within their reach, (the term "stealing" in connection with it appeared to have become obsolete, there, articles looted being viewed in the light of spoils of war.)

While some hunted for relics, others were in pursuit of something to eat, and others, still, would appropriate to themselves anything they could lift, or that "was not nailed down," whether it would be of any use to them or not, and I actually saw one man with more plunder than could be loaded into an ordinary express wagon. One man of our company who had looted a large linen table covering was so afraid that someone would steal it from him, that he made a square package of it and secreted it inside his blouse, which act of his, whether meritorious or otherwise, doubtless was the means of saving a life at Bull Run the next Sunday, when Allen Caswell was wounded in the stomach, the force of the shot being broken by the aforesaid table covering.

Soon after noon matters got quieted down a little. The entire army was at or near Fairfax; guards were posted on all the roads, and an

36

order was issued that any man caught looting or committing any depredation should be committed to Alexandria jail for six months. But I am of the opinion that if the guards had seen one-half the stealing, or heard the dying squeals of those orphan pigs as they were being slain for supper that night, Alexandria's jail would have been a full house, and the fighting force of the army materially reduced.

All the companies of the regiment had one or more men that excelled others not only in their proficiency as soldiers, but they were "professors" in any art or device that tended to add comfort and enjoyment to themselves, particularly when in an enemy's country, and under the necessity of providing their own rations. Just such a man as this we had in our company. James Markham never was known to have an empty haversack, and always managed to procure a full supply of rations, even at times at great personal risk. Just before dark on the afternoon of the day of our occupation of Fairfax, and after the before mentioned order had been given, this man Markham was on guard on a narrow road leading out of the town; on the side of the road where he was pacing was a tight board fence, and on the side opposite a zig-zag, or "Virginia" rail fence. Markham's attention was called by someone to a shoat pig that had all day escaped the "slaughter of the innocents," and was at that moment making the best of his way toward the maternal nest.

The temptation on Markham's part to capture this sprig of porkdom was too mighty to be overcome by any lingering fear of Alexandria's dungeon, so instantly clapping his musket to his shoulder he blazed away, with the result of piggy's dropping in his tracks, without so much as an audible grunt. He sprang out, and had barely secured his prey, when a mounted officer with a squad of cavalry came galloping down the road. Markham proved himself equal to the occasion; quick as thought he tucked the hind legs of the animal underneath his waist-belt behind him, and backing up against the fence, coolly presented arms to the provost guard as they approached, and in reply to the officer's inquiry, "Who fired that shot?" answered, "It was a sentry beyond, down the road." The guard rode on, down the road, but it is presumed they never learned with any degree of accuracy "who fired that shot."

Our company was detailed for picket guard, that night. Brigade guard mount took place in the woods at sunset. Our regimental Band, led by the veteran Joe Greene, played his familiar piece, "The Mocking Bird." Our company was marched in the direction of Leesburg, and posted in the edge of the woods, where picket guard head quarters were established. At about 11 p.m., about one-half of our company relieved a company of the 14th Brooklyn, the balance of the company not going on until 1 a.m. There was occasional firing by the outer picket, or cavalry *vidette*, during the night. General McDowell had his headquarters that night in a covered carriage in the rear of an old blacksmith shop, privates Charles E. Lawton and Silas D. DeBlois, of F Company, being on post near the carriage.

At daylight, July 18th, we were ordered to report to the regiment. The army now started on the road to Centreville, and marched until about 9 a.m., when a halt was ordered. We lay in the road until about 2 p.m., waiting for the divisions on the other roads to come up. At about 3 p.m., firing was heard in the vicinity of Centreville, and we started at once, for some distance going on the double-quick. The occasion of the firing was soon ascertained to be that some of the troops of the First Division having advanced to the vicinity of Blackburn's Ford, were fired upon by the enemy, who were there in force, and after an engagement of about an hour the Union troops fell back, having lost about twenty men.

We continued on our march that afternoon, to near Centreville, where we were ordered to camp. Hunter's entire division were encamped in the fields on both sides of the Warrenton Road, and we were that night given to understand that we would probably remain there a day or two; consequently the next morning, July 19th, we commenced to construct temporary huts of pine trees and boughs for a shelter. That afternoon we had fresh beef sent us in the shape of live cattle, which were distributed to the troops, two to each regiment. Sergeant Major John S. Engs, of our company, asked the privilege of shooting one of these animals, which being granted, he armed himself with a Burnside carbine and fired at about twenty paces, striking the ox in the fore shoulder; the animal started on the run, everybody after him, the sergeant major leading the charge.

The ox, after a chase of half an hour or more, succumbed to exhaustion and was readily despatched; the remaining ox was killed by a man who understood the business. We broiled, fried and stewed our fresh beef that night, and made ourselves as comfortable as possible.

Saturday, July 20th, we loafed around camp, wrote letters home, and visited other camps. At sunset we had dress parade, when orders were read to be in readiness to march at a moment's notice, and for no man to leave his company during the night. Our dress parade was witnessed by General McDowell, his staff and officers, besides officers and men from other regiments; both the Rhode Island regiments were in line. After dress parade the usual religious services, (which were never omitted while in camp,) were held, followed by the singing of the Doxology.

To many who stood at parade rest, that evening, listening, with heads uncovered, to those words of comfort and encouragement from our chaplain, it was to be the last attended on earth, for ere the setting of another sun, they would be lying dead on the fields of Manassas. At tattoo roll-call we were informed by our officers that our regiment would probably march at daylight. The boys rolled their blankets around them, and lying down, secured what little sleep they could, with thoughts busy with the dear ones at home and the probable events of the morrow.

At about 2 a.m. Sunday, 21st, the call sounded, and on every side and in all directions was heard the sound of the bugle and the drum, calling the soldiers from their sleep; and before the echoes of those bugle notes had ceased reverberating among the Virginia hills, our brigade was in line on the road, and ready to move. We were fully assured in our minds that a battle was to be fought that day; in fact Colonel Burnside had the day before stated to our officers that, although the period for which we enlisted had expired, he did not purpose to turn back at such a time, in the face of the enemy, and when the government needed our services; and it is to the credit of the regiment, and the State of Rhode Island, that regardless of the expiration of our term of enlistment we manfully did our duty during that campaign.

The order to march having been given, we tramped steadily along the Warrenton Road, no sounds being heard save the steady tread of the soldiers, and the occasional low words of command from the officers; the stars were still visible, and the nearly full moon was going down behind the western hills. At about daylight we passed through Centreville, and soon arrived at the small bridge at Cub Run. While on the road that morning, we were quite surprised to see Theodore W. King, of our company, join us. He had been quite sick in the hospital at Centreville for two days, but hearing of our regiment passing on the road, he left the hospital and started for his company, saying that if there was any fighting to be done, his place was with Company F. King, though only a mere boy, did his duty manfully on that eventful day, and about noon, in the heat of the battle, fell, mortally wounded.

Just before arriving at Cub Run, we met on the road a regiment and light battery going to the rear. In reply to questions, they said their time was out, and they were going home. This regiment, the 4th Pennsylvania, and the battery of the 8th New York, were the recipients of comments from our men not in the highest degree complimentary to them as men and soldiers, turning back in the face of the enemy, and that must have caused their cheeks to tingle with shame.

The whole three divisions of the army were now in the vicinity of Cub Run. The first division, General Tyler's, was ordered to cross, after doing which these troops advanced along the road to near the Stone Bridge. We crossed Cub Run bridge at 5.30 a.m., after which we struck off to the right through the woods from the main road.

At precisely 6 a.m. the first gun was fired, by Tyler's forces, the object being to engage the enemy's attention while the second division could get into position on the left and rear of their lines. Soon after entering these woods, K and F Companies of the 2nd Rhode Island, and the carbineer company of our regiment, were thrown out as skirmishers. When we entered these woods we had with us a guide, dressed in citizen's clothes, riding a grey horse at the head of the brigade, but after firing began he disappeared from view.

At 10 a.m. we arrived at Sudley Ford, where we were to cross. General McDowell and staff met us, and we were informed by them that the enemy were moving a large force to meet us. After a short halt for the purpose of filling our canteens, we forded the stream. The firing of Tyler's troops could now be distinctly heard. We marched on up the road, past Sudley Church and a number of farm houses; a female standing at the gate of one of these latter made the remark in our hearing that they were all ready for us, and that she hoped we would all be killed before night.

Soon after passing these houses, the 2nd Rhode Island, who were in the advance, continued on in the main road, our regiment branching off into and through a cornfield. Our skirmishers were now engaged with those of the enemy, and driving them back; shells were exploding around and above us as we again came out upon the road. Soon we passed a soldier lying near a fence, wounded. It proved to be William McCann, of K Company, (of Newport) of the 2nd Rhode Island; he had been struck in the head by a fragment of shell, and died soon after. I think he was the first man wounded belonging to our brigade.

Our entire brigade was now halted in a huckleberry pasture, on the edge of some woods. In front of us was a rising ground, of which the enemy apparently had gained possession. Shot and shell were falling among us on every side. The Second Rhode Island, with their battery, were at once ordered to advance toward this rising ground, or hill, and in doing so the enemy opened on them, and for about twenty minutes we stood watching them, with no orders to advance to the assistance of our sister regiment.

At this time the division commander, General Hunter, had been wounded, and Colonel Burnside being the senior Brigadier, took command of the entire division. He at once ordered the 71st New York to the assistance of the 2nd Rhode Island. They advanced a short distance, and then lying down, refused to proceed further, until their two howitzers, which one of their companies were dragging by means of ropes, arrived to their support. Colonel Burnside then gave the command for the 1st Rhode Island to advance. Before moving, we received orders to unsling blankets and haversacks and lay them on the ground at our feet. We marched away and left them, and never saw them again.

We came up in line of battle on the right of the 2nd Regiment and at once commenced firing. Soon the men of F Company that were detailed to serve in the carbineer company joined us; they had been on the skirmish line all the forenoon, but became somewhat mixed when the firing commenced, and were ordered to report to their respective companies. John Rogers was one of the detail, and he was wounded in the leg while running across the field to join us.

Our regiment was so posted, that to preserve the line it was necessary to divide our company by a rail fence, a portion on each side. John P. Peckham was shot in the head and instantly killed, and when he fell, his musket which he was using fell over the fence. Our colour sergeant, Charles Becherer, was shot in the right shoulder and disabled. Albert N. Burdick, 1st colour corporal, then took the flag, and was soon wounded in the arm by a musket ball. At this time Governor Sprague, who was acting as aide for Colonel Burnside, rode through the line to go to the left, when his horse was struck by a rifle ball and fell dead, the Governor going down with him. Captain Tew and Sergeant Sherman went to his assistance, helping him to regain his feet; he was considerably bruised, but not otherwise injured. After two colour bearers had been wounded, the regimental flag was taken and held by Private Robert D. Coggeshall, until, by order of Captain Tew, he was relieved by Private William Hamilton, of the colour guard.

Shot and shell were flying in all directions; we had lost a number of

41

men, and the other companies of the regiment had suffered considerable loss. An officer now rode in front of our regiment and gave the order to cease firing, as we were shooting our own troops. The smoke, which had occasioned this, soon lifted in our front, when we discovered a regiment bearing the union flag marching up the hill in our direction. When a short distance from us, they gave us a volley, which we returned at once, when they turned and retreated down the hill. This regiment was the 4th Alabama, and their colonel, Egbert Jones, was carried to our field hospital, mortally wounded.

With others of our regiment I went over the field after the firing had ceased, and our conclusion was that they were amply repaid for the cruel and unmanly deception practiced upon us. It was never known who the officer was that gave the order to cease firing; he appeared in front of our lines, mounted, with sword uplifted when he gave the order, which was recognized by our company officers, they mistaking him for an *aide-de-camp* or staff officer. It was, however, the opinion of many of the regiment at the time that he was a rebel officer.

Soon the firing in our front ceased. Our ammunition was all expended, we having been under fire for nearly four hours, and had driven the enemy from that portion of the field. This position, from which we had forced the enemy to retire, and which we then held, is known as Buck's Hill, and was regarded as a position of much importance for our forces.

The Third Division had now arrived, and were coming up to our support, and a battalion each of Regular infantry and United States Marines now came up and occupied our position, while our brigade was marched back into the woods for a brief rest and for a fresh supply of ammunition. Having stacked our muskets, the roll was called by the 1st sergeant, and men detailed to look after the dead and wounded. George C. Almy, Christopher Barker and myself were detailed to go for water. Taking as many of the men's canteens as we could carry, we wended our way toward a small, one-story gambrel roof farm house, which was being used by our surgeons as a field hospital, near which was a well of water.

The grounds about the house were covered with wounded and dying men, and it was almost like fighting, to get a supply of water from that well. We however succeeded in filling a portion of our canteens and returned with them to the company. Almost immediately after our arrival back to where the company were resting, the order was given to "fall in." Heavy firing was now again heard on our right, and our officers informed us that the regiment was to change position. Soon troops began to march past us in great confusion; our regiment marched out upon the road and halted. A body of troops passed us headed for the rear, among them two companies of Regular cavalry, whose principal participation in the day's engagement had been the performance of semi-*aide-de-camp* duty.

We were by this time satisfied in our minds that our army was retreating. At this juncture our brigade started back on the road along the edge of the woods, and soon reached the Warrenton road leading to the Stone Bridge. Our regiment preserved good order until they had nearly reached the bridge; the enemy had a battery in position to rake the road over which the retreat was being conducted, and on arriving in proximity to the bridge, we found it to be completely blocked with teams; a large army wagon had, in crossing, been struck by a shell and the horses killed.

The battery of the 2nd Rhode Island Regiment were there, and four of their six guns; after getting one of these over, they dismounted and spiked the remaining three, the men and horses fording the stream. In our regiment it was impossible to preserve order, and ours, like that of the others, became a go-as-you-please march in fording the stream; Governor Sprague strove to halt the regiment and make a stand to beat back the enemy, whereupon Colonel Burnside very promptly informed the Governor, in unmistakable and incontrovertible language, that himself was in command of the 1st Rhode Island Regiment. After crossing, the road branched off to the left, beyond the range of the enemy's fire, and our regiment re-formed and waited until most of the demoralized troops had passed, after which we marched in good order back to our bush camp at Centreville that we had left in the morning, reaching there at 9 p.m., tired, hungry, thirsty and dusty, and many of the regiment wounded.

To add to our general discomfort, a drizzling rain had set in, and we were without blankets, having, as before stated, left them on the field, with our haversacks, before going into action. We, however, lay down in our bush huts, expecting to remain until morning; but about midnight we were aroused and ordered to start on the road to Washington. The drizzle had not abated and the night was dark; we had been in a state of continued and unusual activity since 2 o'clock the previous morning, and in addition had been all day without food. Footsore and weary we started on our march of twenty-six miles to Washington, and soon after daylight, Monday, July 22nd, reached Long

Bridge, where we made a halt and rations were served to us, and at 8 a.m. we crossed over to Washington, and marched across the city to our old home at Camp Sprague. The roll was called, a ration of whiskey was given us, and all turned in for a much needed and well earned rest.

OPINIONS ON THE BATTLE

Many opinions have been given as to the causes that led to the defeat of the Union army at Bull Run. General Sherman, who commanded a brigade in the battle, said it was the best planned and worst fought battle of the war. It has been said by some writers that the plans of the commanding general were not carried out, and that each of the three division commanders whose forces were actually engaged acted on their own responsibility and were governed by circumstances. It is a fact well known today, that the Union army, at or in the vicinity of the battle field, were in numbers quite sufficient to have at least held any and every position that a portion of the army had gained.

On a map now in possession of Charles E. Lawton Post, G. A. R. of this city, of Bull Run battlefield, drawn under the direction of Generals McDowell and Beauregard, by order of the War Department, the position of every regiment and brigade of both armies at the commencement of the engagement is defined, and in a note appended to the map it is stated that the engagement was commenced by the Burnside brigade, and it is a historical fact recognized at this time, that the battle was fought and won by the Second Division, commanded by Burnside, General Hunter having been wounded before the troops had been brought into position, supported by no other troops, until noon, when a brigade of the Third Division, which had followed us through the forest road, came to our assistance.

From 9.30 a.m. to 1 p.m., these seventeen regiments of infantry and four light batteries, unaided by any other troops, fought and drove the enemy from their position on Buck's Hill; and when the two brigades of Tyler's First Division, commanded by Generals Sherman and Schenck, crossed Bull Run river, over Stone Bridge, at 1.30 p.m., there was not a rebel force of any description on the north side of Warrenton road, west of Stone Bridge. At this time victory was assured for the Union army. At the Stone Bridge was Tyler's entire division, comprising fifteen regiments of infantry and three batteries, the Fourth Division, General Runyon, with seven regiments, Fifth Division, General Miles, eight regiments, and one battery.

Of these thirteen thousand men, only two brigades of the First Division crossed the river in the afternoon, and they were engaged only about one hour, namely, in the vicinity of the Henry House, when they were repulsed by the enemy, whose forces were now all concentrated at that point. Rickett's Regular battery (formerly Magruder's stationed at Fort Adams previous to the war) was lost, recaptured, and lost again. These two brigades of the First Division retreated, panic stricken, and our reserve of twelve thousand men, at Stone Bridge, retreated without firing a shot, while our Division, the 2nd, was holding the position we had gained in the morning.

This was the supreme moment, when a Sheridan or a Warren would have swept the opposing forces from the field, or captured their entire army. Colonel Burnside, seeing the aspect matters had assumed, formed his troops into line and fell back to the Warrenton road, fearing he might be cut off at Stone Bridge. Hunter's division covered the retreat and were the last troops that crossed the bridge, and was the only division of the army that occupied its former quarters, as these did, at Centreville that night.

DAY AFTER THE BATTLE

The day after the battle was a busy one in camp; men were straggling in all day, some of them that we had left among the wounded at the field hospital on our departure the evening previous, who had managed to hobble along on the road, and after a while reached camp. Some of these, owing to the darkness of the night, had taken the wrong road from Fairfax and brought up at Alexandria, whence they set out anew, reaching Long Bridge and the camp some hours later. Among these latter was John Fludder, who did not arrive until Monday afternoon, when he surprised us by bringing with him the regimental flag, which we had supposed to have been lost when the regiment "straggled" at Stone Bridge, as no one could give any information in regard to it. Fludder found it where it had been dropped in the confusion of retreat, and in order to save it tore it from the staff and secreting it about his person, thus brought it in. Samuel Hilton, who had been left on the field for dead, also came straggling in; he had been hit in the temple by a partially spent fragment of a shell and laid out senseless and inanimate, and was afterwards revived by the drizzling rain, as were also quite a number belonging to other regiments.

Company F had its full share of losses in killed and wounded. The first man of the company wounded was John B. Landers, shot through the wrist; then followed John Rogers, shot in the leg, Charles Becherer, colour sergeant, wounded in the shoulder, Albert N. Burdick, colour corporal, wounded in the arm, John P. Peckham, shot in the head and killed, Andrew P. Bashford, shot in the breast and taken prisoner, Theodore W. King, shot through the groin, mortally wounded, taken prisoner, and afterwards died in Philadelphia, when on his way home, Thomas J. Harrington, shot in the head and killed, Allen Caswell, shot in the stomach, Henry T. Easton, wounded in the arm, Samuel Hilton, wounded as above stated, Bartlett L. Simmons, taken prisoner, Robert Crane, never accounted for, but supposed to have been killed during the retreat.

July 24th, Doctor David King and Alderman James C. Powell, of Newport, arrived in camp. Doctor King obtained a pass through the lines for the purpose of attending his son, wounded as above stated, and who was a prisoner in Richmond. Alderman Powell was deputed by the city government of Newport to look after the sick and wounded of Company F on their way home.

Orders were received, July 24th, to make preparations for return to Rhode Island, as our term of service had expired. Colonel Burnside offered the services of the regiment for a longer time, as it was expected that the rebels would make an attack on Washington; but it was thought our services would not be needed, and preparations for departure were accordingly made. On Thursday, July 25th, we had dress parade for the last time in Washington. After the parade, the 2nd Regiment was formed in line directly opposite and facing us, and the men of the two regiments exchanged muskets, each with the man opposite him; the muskets of the Second were old, smooth bore, altered over, while those of the First were the latest improved Springfield rifles. During the evening, we improved the opportunity to visit the camp of the Second, bidding them good bye, and receiving such messages and tokens as they desired to send home to friends.

CHAPTER 6

"Home, Sweet Home"

At 9 p.m., 25th, the command was given to "Fall in;" the line was formed, we marched into the city, and at midnight bid farewell to Washington, the cars taking us into Baltimore at daylight, where we waited on the streets all the forenoon for the special train that was to take us to Philadelphia. We got away from Baltimore at 2 p.m., arriving in Philadelphia in the evening. We had been expected, and were entertained by the citizens with a fine collation at the New England rooms.

We left that city at 2 a.m., July 27th, arriving in New York soon after daylight, where the regiment embarked on board steamers *Bay State* and *State of Maine*, for Providence. Each steamer took five companies, ours being on the *State of Maine*, on board of which we were given a nice breakfast. We steamed out of New York at about 11 a.m., July 27th, the transports proceeding slowly to avoid arriving in Providence at a late hour in the day. At 10.30 p.m. we were off Beaver Tail light; F Company was called and formed on the hurricane deck, Captain Tew arranging with the steamer captain to sail through the inner harbour of Newport. When opposite Fort Greene, a squad of the Newport artillery fired a salute, which was answered with cheering by F Company, and the blowing of the steamer's whistle. Both steamers proceeded up the bay and anchored, it being the wish to not land before daylight.

At 6 a.m. Sunday, July 28th, landed, and, escorted by the militia of the state, marched through the city to Railroad Hall, Exchange Place, where a substantial breakfast awaited us. After breakfast and speeches by Bishop Clark and others, the regimental companies residing outside of Providence were ordered to their homes, to report again in Providence August 2nd.

F Company, escorted by the past members of the Newport Artillery, Colonel Fludder in command, and the Old Guard, both of which companies had that morning come from Providence to receive us, left for Newport on steamer Perry at 11 a.m., arriving at Sayer's Wharf in Newport, at 1 p.m.

On our arrival we found the wharf and streets of the city through which we were to pass crowded with people of all ages and both sexes, as though the whole of Newport had turned out to greet us. Services were omitted by the churches, all evidently regarding it as a duty appropriate to the Sabbath to welcome to their homes those who had gone forth to peril their lives at their country's call. Tears dropped from many eyes, as those were remembered who had left home with us, but would never return.

We marched up Thames street, our sick and wounded in carriages, through Touro street and Bellevue Avenue, to Touro Park, where we were welcomed in addresses by Mayor Cranston and other city officials. On invitation of Mr. William Newton, proprietor of the Atlantic house, we partook of an excellent dinner at that hostelry, after which a short street parade was made to the armoury on Clarke street, where we were dismissed, with orders to report again on the 2nd of August.

On Friday, August 2nd, we reported at the armoury and proceeded to Providence; we received our pay and were mustered out of the United States service, by Colonel Loomis, of the 5th United States Infantry. In the afternoon a final parade was made by the entire regiment, but F Company were obliged to leave the line before its conclusion, in order to take the 5 p.m. boat for home.

A few days after the arrival home of the company, a beautiful set of flags was received by Mayor Cranston, a gift from Rhode Islanders residing in California to the colour company of the 1st Rhode Island Regiment, and were accompanied by the following explanatory letter:

San Francisco, Cal., Aug. 30, 1861.

Hon. Wm. H. Cranston, Mayor City Newport:—

Sir,—At a meeting of the natives and citizens of Rhode Island now residents of California, we, the undersigned, were appointed a committee to forward to your Honour a set of regimental colours for the First Rhode Island Regiment, to be by you presented to them in person as a token of our esteem and admiration for the prompt, noble and efficient response made by them to the patriotic call of our country to fight for constitutional liberty, and for the brave, honourable and veteran-like manner in which they have performed their duties.

Very Respectfully, your obedient servants,

William Sherman,
E. P. Peckham,
Jas. M. Olney,
B. H. Randolph,
C. V. S. Gibbs.

On Tuesday, October 29th, 1861, a formal presentation of the flags to Company F took place on Touro Park. The company were present in good numbers, and Colonel Burnside was also present by invitation. Mayor Cranston, after reading the correspondence accompanying the flags, remarked as follows:

"Company F, accept this offering—our unconquered and unconquerable national flag—and this State standard, the emblem of freedom for more than two hundred years—the patriotic and cheerful gift of Rhode Islanders in the Eden of the Pacific to you, their brothers in the Eden of the Atlantic. Guard them sacredly and well—carefully preserve and affectionately cherish them; if necessary, lay down your lives in their defence against foreign invasion or domestic insurrection, and your reward will be the gratitude of honest and loyal men on earth, the approbation of God, and eternal felicity in that new Paradise where there will neither be wars nor rumours of wars, and where the King of Kings and the Prince of Peace will reign supreme forever."

Colonel Burnside responded. After a few remarks acknowledging the kindness of the patriotic Californians, he turned to the members of Company F and addressed them as follows:

With you, Company F, I leave these colours. For their proper keeping I need give you no charge. You have been tried and have indeed been found not wanting. Take them; accept them as a part of the history of the First Rhode Island Regiment, as a part of the history of your own gallant state and as an emblem of the glory of your dearly loved country. Love the one flag and revere the others. Many dark hours we have already passed through, and many more are yet to be undergone. But let no man of us falter as to the success of our glorious cause. In all our work, however dangerous or arduous, we shall be followed by the prayers of loved friends at home and of the true and loyal of all our country, and of the good and true of every land.

The great God above may chasten us in his wisdom, but rest assured He will never forsake us in His justice. To you, Mr. Mayor, I render my sincere thanks for your kind words of me. They are indeed precious to me. The words of commendation which have been spoken of my conduct by my approving fellow citizens are my highest reward. And as to Company F, I have no fears but they will do as they have done before—their whole duty. Better soldiers never trod the soil of this or any other land. Not a man of them failed to execute my orders to the letter. Never soldiers did their duty—their whole duty—more promptly or gallantly. Take these beautiful flags, Company F, take them and keep them; you have the well earned right to keep them. Twice was your own flag stricken down in the field of battle and then a third man from your ranks seized it and it was borne aloft in safety from the field though pierced with many bullets.

Then turning to the mayor, he added:

And in conclusion allow me to thank you, sir, and all concerned in this presentation, for this beautiful gift to Rhode Island's first and gallant regiment.

Company F then made a parade through the city, displaying the flags.

At a meeting held by Company F at the armoury of the Artillery Company, November 5th, 1861, it was voted to place the flags in charge of three members of Company F, and Corporal Tayer and Privates DeBlois and Terrell were appointed that committee, with instructions to place them in the Newport city hall for safe keeping. It was soon afterwards ascertained that the place allotted to them in the city hall was damp, and it was decided to remove them to a place where they would be better preserved, and could be seen at any time. The place selected was the Artillery Company's armoury, where they were suitably mounted, and will doubtless always remain.

Soon after the muster out of F Company, recruiting commenced at once for new regiments from Rhode Island, and of 108 officers and men composing Company F at muster out, 84 re-entered the service either in the army or navy, many of them occupying positions of rank in both branches of the service during the war.

Conclusion

Company F, 1st Rhode Island Regiment, is a thing of the past. Thirty years have come and gone since the enactment of the stirring scenes in which we participated; but those scenes and incidents still exist in the minds and memories of the men composing that company. A large portion of its members have left the city, and many have been carried to that silent camp where they "sleep their last sleep, have fought their last battle; no sound can awake them to glory again." But as each succeeding 17th of April rolls around, the surviving members of the company meet to talk over the incidents of the long ago, tell stories of camp and field, and say a word of those who have left us to return no more; and we shall continue these gatherings at least once a year, until the last man of Company F shall have been mustered out to join those who have gone before.

History of Company E of the 6th Minnesota Regiment of Volunteer Infantry

Alfred J. Hill

ALFRED J. HILL

Contents

Preface

It will be remembered by those connected with the military service that towards the end of the late Civil War, there went through the camps and barracks of the volunteer soldiers agents of publishing houses busily engaged in procuring material for "company histories," and still more anxiously soliciting subscriptions for the same. These histories were mere broadsides or charts, giving the name and rank of each man, with a few other personal facts, compiled from the muster rolls, and in addition an abstract of campaign movements, battles, and so forth; all the information being brought up to date of subscription. Of course as permanent and final records such publications would be failures, there being no "next" in which to "conclude" their stories.

While the Sixth Minnesota Infantry Regiment lay at New Orleans, one of the visitations described occurred to it (this being a very successful one), and thereupon a member of Company E proposed to a comrade the getting up of something of the kind among themselves, to be of home manufacture. Time permitting, the work was then commenced, continued in the field, and kept up with current events till the order for return home of the command to which the company belonged. Serious illness of the compiler, and the scattering of the members of the company, prevented the finishing of the work at the intended time, and caused its indefinite postponement.

As a contribution, though humble, to material for some future history of the part taken by Minnesota in the war for the Union this little book has been completed and published, and the writer would be greatly pleased if its appearance should stimulate the necessary research for the putting on record in somewhat similar form of the histories of other companies of our state regiments.

Alfred J. Hill.
St. Paul, Minn., 1869.

PART 1

Origin and Organization—1862

In the spring of 1862 a sixth regiment of infantry had been called for from Minnesota by the Governor of the State, but, from various causes, the enlistments proceeded very languidly till the disasters of the Virginian armies in the summer and the consequent proclamations of the President of the United States for volunteers gave an immense impulse to recruiting.

Under such circumstances it was that the "Sigel Guards," afterwards Company E of the Sixth Regiment, were projected and raised. In the month of June, Mathias Holl, of St. Paul, was authorized to recruit for the proposed company; and on the 23rd of July, twenty men having been enlisted, he received a regular recruiting commission. Rudolph Schoenemann and Christian Exel, of the same city, also engaged in the work in connection with Lieutenant Holl, themselves enlisting in the company on the 6th and 14th of August, respectively. Many of the members, however, were not obtained particularly by these gentlemen, some having been recruited for other companies or regiments and transferred involuntarily to the Sigel Guards, others who had purposed enlisting in other companies—that never were filled—having joined it of their own accord, while a large proportion acted as their own recruiting officers, and made it their first choice.

The names of those recruited for, or who intended to join, other organizations, are as follows, *viz.*: (1) Beckendorf, Besecke, Detert, Gropel, Mahle, Mann, Metz, J. J. Mueller, Schaefer, Simon, and Temme, were to have belonged to the company projected by Messrs. Klinkenfus, Knauft, and Krueger, of Lower Town, St. Paul. They joined in a body. (2) Bast, Blesius, Blessner, Dreis, Fandel, Greibler, Hoscheid, and Neierburg were enlisted August 15th by Messrs. Julius Gross and Lieutenant Kreitz, of St. Paul, for the Tenth Regiment, but were transferred to the Sixth. (3) George Paulson, a recruit for L. C. Dayton's company (St. Paul) for the Eighth Regiment, was transferred to the Sixth. (4) John, Kilian, Kraemer, Meyer, Praxl, and Radke came to Fort Snelling from Winona, as recruits for the Seventh Regiment, but enlisted instead in the Sigel Guards. All the recruits were enlisted and sworn in as privates except the drummer, the period of enlistment being "for three years unless sooner discharged."

The general rendezvous was at Fort Snelling, and, the "minimum" number (83) having been obtained, the company was provisionally organized there, on the 16th of August, by the enlisted men expressing, by vote, their preference for candidates to fill the commissioned offices, and by the captain, then chosen, appointing the non-commissioned officers. Schoenemann and Holl were thus respectively elected captain and second lieutenant of the Sigel Guards, and were commissioned as such, on the 19th, by the Governor of the State, and Lieutenant Exel, already commissioned (August 11th), accepted as first lieutenant.

By the 19th of August the aggregate number of members was 94; their names, rank, etc., being shown in the following roll:

NAME	NATIVE COUNTRY	When Enlisted 1862
OFFICERS.		
Captain—		
*Rudolph Schoenemann	Prussia	Aug. 14
First Lieutenant—		
Christian Exel	Hesse Darmstadt	Aug. 6
Second Lieutenant—		
Mathias Holl	Hesse Darmstadt	July 23
First Sergeant—		
Justus B. Bell	Ohio	Aug. 4
Second Sergeant—		
George Huhn	Bavaria	Aug. 7
Third Sergeant—		
*Frederick Scheer	Prussia	July 23
Fourth Sergeant—		
Ernst J. Knobelsdorff	Prussia	July 29
Fifth Sergeant—		
*Elias Siebert	Hesse Cassel	Aug. 2
First Corporal—		
*Paul P. Huth	Prussia	June 13
Second Corporal—		
John Burch	Prussia	Aug. 13

Third Corporal—		
*Mathias Mueller	Prussia	Aug. 5
Fourth Corporal—		
*William Rohde	Hesse Cassel	Aug. 2
Fifth Corporal—		
Peter Leitner	Bavaria	Aug. 6
Sixth Corporal—		
Reinhard Stiefel	Prussia	Aug. 7
Seventh Corporal—		
George Sauer	Bavaria	Aug. 7
Eighth Corporal—		
Richard Mueller	Prussia	Aug. 8
Musician—		
*Charles Seidel	Prussia	July 9
Privates—		
Bast, William	Luxemburg	Aug. 15
Beckendorf, Peter H.	Prussia	Aug. 14
Becker, Mathias	Prussia	Aug. 13
Besecke, Ferdinand	Prussia	Aug. 14
Blesius, John	Prussia	Aug. 15
Blessner, Charles	Luxemburg	Aug. 15
Boos, Michael	Bavaria	June 12
Bristle, Christian	Baden	Aug. 4
Detert, Henry	Prussia	Aug. 14
Dreis, Nicholas	Luxemburg	Aug. 15
*Eberdt, Charles	Mecklenb	Aug. 13
Eheim, Joseph	Austria	Aug. 14
Fandel, Henry	Luxemburg	Aug. 15
*Ferlein, Joseph	Bavaria	June 2
Fischer, Louis	Switzerland	Aug. 16
Gaheen, Samuel	Canada	Aug. 14
*Gantner, Jacob	Switzerland	June 10
Goldner, Joseph	Prussia	July 23
Griebler, Joseph	Prussia	Aug. 15
*Gropel, Henry	Prussia	Aug. 14
Hahn, F. Carl	Wurtemberg	July 23
Harrfeldt, August	Holstein	July 28
Hauck, Jacob	Baden	Aug. 14
*Hellmann, Herman	Prussia	Aug. 9
Henricks, Frederick	Prussia	July 28
Henricks, Henry	Prussia	Aug. 5
Hill, Alfred J.	England	Aug. 14
Hill, William A.	Virginia	July 22
Hoscheid, Nicholas	Luxemburg	Aug. 15

Jakobi, Conrad	Hesse Darmstadt	July 18
John, Jacob	Bremen	Aug. 18
*Juergens, Louis	Waldeck	Aug. 16
*Kellermann, August	Prussia	Aug. 14
Kernen, Jacob	Switzerland	Aug. 14
Kilian, Philip	Hesse Darmstadt	Aug. 18
*Klinghammer, Louis	Prussia	July 9
*Kobelitz, Frederick	Bremen	July 28
*Koenig, Louis	Baden	Aug. 12
*Kraemer, Frederick	Wurtemberg	Aug. 18
*Krueger, Henry	Schleswig	Aug. 15
Mahle, William	Wurtemberg	Aug. 14
Mann, Jacob	Wurtemberg	Aug. 14
*Martin, Frederick	Prussia	Aug. 16
Metz, Charles	Hanover	Aug. 14
Maurer, John J.	Prussia	Aug. 13
Meyer, John H.	Ohio	Aug. 18
Mueckenhausen, Joseph	Prussia	Aug. 14
Mueckenhausen, Mathias	Prussia	Aug. 14
Mueller, John Jacob	Wurtemberg	Aug. 14
Munson, John	Sweden	June 26
Neierburg, Michael	Luxemburg	Aug. 15
Parks, Thomas M.	Pennsylvania	June 13
*[1]Paulson, George	Prussia	July 28
Paulson, Paul	Norway	June 10
Peterson, Ole	Norway	July 28
Porth, William	Prussia	Aug. 7
Praxl, Anthony A.	Austria	Aug. 18
Radke, Rudolph	Prussia	Aug. 18
Rehse, August	Prussia	Aug. 4
*Reimers, Joachim	Holstein	Aug. 13
*Reuter, Henry	Hanover	July 23
Rossion, Jean	Belgium	July 31
Schafer, Henry	Canada	Aug. 14
Schauer, August	Prussia	Aug. 4
Scheibel, Augustin	France	Aug. 15
Schene, William	Hanover	Aug. 12
Schermann, George	Austria	Aug. 11
Schoenheiter, Frederick	Prussia	Aug. 16
Simon, John	Prussia	Aug. 14
Smith, Joseph	France	Aug. 14
Smith, William A.	Indiana	Aug. 19

1. This young man's real name was Paul Bierstach, the other having been assumed to enable him to get sworn in without his parents' consent.

Sproesser, William D.	Wurtemberg	July 23
Stengelin, Gottfried	Wurtemberg	July 16
	Prussia	Aug. 14
Wetteran, Louis	Wisconsin	Aug. 5
Willialms, August	Sweden	June 10
*Wolf, Anton	Prussia	June 2

* In military service before.

With the exception of less than half a dozen, all of the above were residents of Minnesota, fifty-four being from St. Paul, eight from Winona, and the remainder from other parts of the state. Twenty-four of the members had been soldiers previously, many of them having seen active service—seventeen in European armies, one in the United States regulars, and six in the United States volunteer forces. Wolf—then a boy of sixteen—enlisted in Bulow's Army Corps, fought at Quatre Bras, and was present at the battle of Waterloo.

PART 2.

Services In Minnesota Against the Sioux Indians—1862-63

Immediately after the organization of the company the usual recruit life began. Military clothing and equipments were issued, squad drill commenced, and light guard duty done in and around the fort. The quarters of the company were two rooms on the northern side of the parade grounds, with a kitchen and dining room below. Fritz Stirneman, a civilian, but an ex-soldier of the First Regiment, assisted by Rossion, was hired to do the cooking.

The monotony of barrack life, however, did not last long. The news of the outbreak of the Sioux Indians in the western part of the state turned all thoughts from anticipations of Southern campaigns to the necessities of the hour. The regiment was put on a war footing, orders to march were issued, and arms and accoutrements supplied to the men; four Sibley tents being allowed for the enlisted men of each company. On the 20th of August the first battalion of the Sixth Regiment, consisting of three companies, left Fort Snelling for the scene of the massacre, and, together with Company A, which had been ordered to march across the country, arrived at St. Peter on the 22nd. All being ready, the second battalion, including Company E, embarked on the evening of the 22nd, on the steamboat *Wilson* for the upper Minnesota River. At the time of embarkation the aggregate strength of the company was 94, the number present being 84; the absentees being Lieutenant Exel, on recruiting service; John, Harrfeldt, Kraemer, Martin, Meyer, Praxl, and Radke, on furlough; Dreis and Fandel, who had not yet joined; and Porth, left behind at the fort on account of inability to march.

On the morning of the 23rd we disembarked at Shakopee, 24

miles from the fort. From this day commenced the official organization of the regiment, it being the date of Colonel William Crooks' commission. The route followed was through Jordan, Belle Plaine, and Henderson, to St. Peter, where we arrived on the 24th. All the companies of the Sixth were now concentrated at this point, where an expeditionary force was collecting for the relief of Fort Ridgley, then sorely pressed by the Indians. On the 26th the expedition commenced the march, and arrived at the fort on the 28th; the regiment encamping on the prairie nearby.

H. Henricks was appointed wagoner of the company on the 30th. Also on that day Louis Thiele, a Prussian settler of the neighbourhood, whose family had been murdered by the Indians, enlisted in the company as a private.

On the 31st an expedition under the command of Major Joseph E. Brown, consisting of the Union Guards (Company A), under Captain Grant, and a detail of men from the other companies of the Sixth Regiment, and the Cullen Guards under Captain Anderson, was dispatched to the Lower Agency to bury the dead, and ascertain if possible the position of the enemy.

Early on the morning of September 2nd, rapid firing was heard in the direction of the Agency. The scouts reported that the detachment under Major Brown was attacked and surrounded at Birch Coolie, twenty miles from the fort and three miles from the Lower Agency. A second detachment under Colonel McPhail, consisting of the Hickory Guards (Company B), Sigel Guards (Company E), Young Men's Guard (Company G), of the Sixth Regiment, under Major McLaren, also some cavalry and one howitzer under Captain Mark Hendricks, was at once sent forward to their relief.

When within three miles of the beleaguered force, the demonstrations of the Indians became so threatening—coming near enough to shoot one of the horses—that the commander of the relieving party, not daring to fight his way through, made a halt, had the horses unhitched, and disposed the men to meet the expected attack, but, as the enemy did not return any nearer to us, we shortly fell back some distance to a better position. Night soon came on and it was spent watchfully by the men behind their corralled wagons, the silence being broken only by the occasional firing of the howitzer. The firing had been heard at the fort and towards morning the little force was strengthened by the arrival of the remainder of the Sixth Regiment, the Seventh Regiment, which had just arrived at the fort, and two pieces of artillery.

About daylight on the 3rd, the combined forces were drawn up in line of battle, ready to move; the Indians soon appeared and commenced the attack, but the return fire was so heavy, and evidently so unexpected, that they almost immediately retreated to the woods in the coolie, from which they were driven by the heavy fire delivered by the artillery. The Indians having been repulsed, the whole force continued their march to Birch Coolie camp, and the Indians then abandoned the attack of the party there, though the soldiers of the first relieving party were not allowed the honour of driving them, which was given to the Seventh Regiment. After burying the dead and attending to the wounded, the troops returned to their camp at Fort Ridgley.

Five men of the company were with the original detachment at the battle of Birch Coolie. R. Mueller and Klinghammer were severely wounded, the former in the side and arm, and the latter in the leg. They were cared for at the post hospital. Dreis and Fandel were there, having accompanied the volunteer cavalry from St. Paul; Dreis joined on the 4th and Fandel, being wounded in the hand, went to the hospital. Thiele, too, was present at this fight. About this time Lieutenant Exel with the seven furloughed Winona men returned.

Shortly after this affair the order of the adjutant general of the state was received and published, fixing the letters of the companies according to the rank of the respective captains. The Sigel Guards were the fifth company, and so became E; in position it was therefore the seventh from the right wing of the regiment, and had, when marching during the summer, Company A of the Ninth Regiment in front, and Company K of the Sixth in the rear.

While preparations for the campaign were progressing, the troops were drilled daily in the "school of the soldier" and "of the company;" and, among other things, trenches were dug at the fort, and beyond the camps. About the middle of the month Eberdt was detailed as regimental pioneer.

On the 18th of the month the expeditionary force took up the line of march from its base at Fort Ridgley. Crossing at the ferry nearby, the route pursued was on the south side of the Minnesota River, fording the Red Wood at the usual place, and touching Wood Lakes, about three miles from Yellow Medicine, which was reached on the 22nd. On the morning of the 23rd the Indians surprised a foraging party half a mile distant from the camp. The Third Regiment formed in line, and, crossing a ravine, opened fire on the Indians, but immediately received orders to fall back. The Third recrossed the ravine, and, the Renville Rangers coming to their support, the Indian advance was checked. Captain Hendricks placed his artillery in a raking position at the head of the ravine, and soon dislodged the enemy.

On the right, Colonel Marshall with five companies of the Seventh Regiment, and Companies A and I of the Sixth under Lieutenant Colonel Averill, charged and drove the Indians from their position. On the left, a similar flank movement was repelled by Major McLaren with Companies F and K of the Sixth, while the remainder of the regiment was held in reserve. The action lasted about two hours, at the end of which time, the Indians being unable to withstand the murderous fire of shot and shell rained upon them, fled with great precipitation, and thus ended the battle of Wood Lake.

The whole plan of battle seems to have been of defence, fought on the old lines of chivalry—man for man, instead of bringing all the troops in line of action and dealing the enemy a crushing blow at the beginning. This mode of action may have been very nice from an Indian's point of view, but the men in the reserve who stood in line of battle for nearly two hours, and those engaged at the front who were held back and not allowed to drive the enemy, would have preferred a little less chivalry and a few more dead Indians.

On the 25th the line of march was again taken up, and on the 26th we arrived at the camp of the "so-called" friendly Indians, where were most of the white captives taken during the insurrection, and who in a day or two were delivered up. This place was nearly opposite the mouth of the Chippewa River, and nearby, about a quarter of a mile south of the Minnesota River, was formed the camp ever afterwards to be known in local history as Camp Release, from this memorable surrender of captives there.

On the 4th of October, Captain Whitney, with two companies of the Sixth and one from the Seventh, was sent below in charge of the Indian prisoners to gather the crops in the vicinity of the Yellow Medicine Agency. On the 5th all the company present, 91 in number, were mustered into the military service of the United States, "for three years from their respective dates of enrolment." On the 13th, Colonel Marshall was sent to the westward with a detachment consisting of Company G of the Sixth Regiment, 100 men of the Third, and one howitzer, in quest of the Indians reported to be near the headwaters of the Lac qui Parle River and Two Lakes (Mde-nonpana) in the

Coteaus. The expedition returned on the 21st, having penetrated the prairies nearly to the James River, and having in charge about 150 Indian prisoners, including men, women and children.

By company order of September 22nd, Corporal Huth was promoted to fifth sergeant, and Privates J. Smith and Martin appointed seventh and eighth corporals, respectively. On October 13th warrants bearing the same date were made out and signed by the colonel for all the non-commissioned officers, making the grades agree with said order, but causing them to take effect from the 18th of August. On the 14th Company F left for Yellow Medicine to reinforce Captain Whitney. On the night of the 15th, Captain Merriman, with Company B and 35 mounted men (including 25 scouts), made a raid beyond the lower Lac qui Parle, and captured 23 lodges, in all 67 Indians. On the 18th W. A. Hill rejoined. While at Camp Release the duty performed was chiefly guarding the Indian prisoners, foraging, and serving on camp guard,—a very strict and irksome one. Company drill in the morning and battalion drill in the afternoon were also required.

Though within sixty miles of depots of supplies, and though the majority of the fighting men of the insurgent Indians had either been captured, or had surrendered, or retreated further up the Minnesota river, the rank and file of this small army had here to suffer for the want of commissary stores,—truly following the advice of the ancient philosopher to leave off eating with yet a little appetite. Had it not been for the potatoes of the Indian gardens and cattle of the slaughtered and fugitive settlers—which provisions, though costing nothing to the government at the time, were made to offset the amounts due for non-issued rations, the source of "company funds"—we would have been nearly starved.

The return march was begun on the 23rd of October, on which day the weather turned suddenly cold and a high wind rose, which blew down many of the tents at Yellow Medicine that night. Arrived at the Lower Agency on the 25th, and then went into camp at Camp Sibley; and remained there till the 8th of November, and then resumed the march. The next day the company was detailed as guard for the prisoners, two men being assigned to each wagon. Though the troops left the village of New Ulm a mile or more to the left, yet the citizens, exasperated at the sight of the Indians in the wagons guarded by the soldiers, lined the road opposite the town in great excitement, hurling stones and endeavouring to get at the Indians, in which they partly succeeded. On the 10th we arrived at Blue Earth

River bridge, and camped a little beyond it, on the town site of Le Hillier (L'Huillier) and immediately south of the isolated bluff at the mouth of the river,—the camp being called Camp Lincoln.

Here Eberdt was relieved. Fischer left on the 15th on furlough, from which he never returned; Juergens and Knobelsdorff, sick, were sent to the hospital at Mankato the same day. Gaheen, Gantner, Meyer and Parks had been detailed or detached as regimental teamsters during parts of October and November, but by this time were all with the company again for duty.

The regiment marched, by the way of Mankato, to St. Peter, on the 17th, having travelled to the latter place, since leaving Fort Snelling in August, as a regiment of the expeditionary brigade, about 350 miles. The campaign being terminated, the companies departed to their various assigned winter stations,—Companies A, B, G, H, and K for Fort Snelling; D for Forest City; E for Hutchinson, McLeod county; and C, F, and I for Glencoe. Lieutenant Holl was detailed as quartermaster and commissary for the company during its separation from the regiment.

On the 18th of November we left St. Peter with Companies C, D, and F: four miles beyond New Auburn parted with C and F, and with D at Hutchinson, where we arrived on the 20th. This place was already garrisoned by Company B of the Ninth Regiment, quartered in good log houses, but there was no accommodation for the newly-arrived company, and fatigue parties had at once to be set to work cutting and hauling logs for building. The season, however, being too far advanced, the work was abandoned, permission having been obtained to hire quarters at Kingston instead. On the 24th Dreis died of diphtheria. He was buried in the village burial-grounds nearby. Seven men had to be left at Hutchinson on departure,—five sick and two as nurses.

On the 28th we left for Kingston, travelling by the way of Greenleaf, Round Lake, and Forest City, and reaching destination the next day. An old frame store near the mill on the west bank of the Crow River was used for barrack purposes, and by the erection of a log kitchen and bake house, with some other improvements, served the purpose very well. Duties were light, provisions good and ample in quantity, and the time passed pleasantly enough. A system of furloughs was inaugurated, and every man had the privilege of fifteen days' leave of absence. After the departure of Fischer, Koenig had to cook alone, and when he went on furlough, December 16th, Gantner and Rossion conducted the kitchen in the interim. Sergeant Burch left on furlough on the 16th, but being detailed in St. Paul at District Headquarters he did not return to the company at the expiration of his leave of absence; also Griebler, who did not return to Kingston either. Sergeant Scheer was reduced to the ranks at his own request on the 20th, and on the same day Corporal Burch was, by company order, promoted to fifth sergeant; also privates Neierburg and Eheim were appointed, respectively, seventh and eighth corporals, on the 4th of January, 1863, to fill vacancies, the enlisted men having shown their preferences by special election; the same day also Gaheen and Hauck were similarly recommended for company cooks, and were detailed as such. Juergens rejoined on the 13th. A. J. Hill left for Washington, D.C., in obedience to orders from the Headquarters of the Army requiring him to report there for duty; same day John left on furlough, but, becoming ill, did not return to the company at its expiration. Sproesser was detailed as company fifer on February 1st. Klinghammer rejoined, sick, on the 6th; he having been mustered in at Fort Ridgley on the 13th of October.

The company being ordered to Fort Snelling, where the headquarters of the regiment were, left Kingston on the 27th of February, on the arrival of Company H, which relieved it, and travelled, in sleighs mostly, by the way of Clear Water and Dayton, reaching the fort on the 1st of March. Quarters were assigned it in the old barracks, near the sutler's store, and the usual routine of drill and guard duty began again. Here Fandel joined, sick, and Griebler rejoined. Jakobi was detailed as company bugler on the 22nd, and John rejoined on the 29th. Private Kobelitz was on the 1st of April honourably discharged, for disability.

The regiment went into camp on the river, about a mile above the fort, on the 4th, and Sibley tents were issued as before. George Paulson left on detached service for Yellow Medicine on the 12th, afterwards (in June) acting as orderly at regimental headquarters. William Gabbert, a Prussian, resident of St. Paul, enlisted as private in the company on the 13th. Privates Griebler and Maurer left on the 17th on a (forged) pass, but did not return at the proper time, and were afterwards found to have deserted. Privates Harrfeldt, W. A. Hill, and Meyer were, by District order of the 1st of May, transferred to the Third Minnesota Battery.

PART 3

Indian Campaign in Minnesota and Dakota–1863-64

At the end of April, 1863, orders were received to rendezvous at Camp Pope on the upper Minnesota River. Fifteen of the men had to be left behind at the fort, *viz.*: J. J. Mueller and Reimers, on detached service; and Becker, Fandel, Gantner, John, Kellermann, Knobelsdorff, Koenig, Mann, J. Mueckenhausen, Peterson, Schauer, Scheer, and Wolf, sick. On the 28th of April Companies E and D embarked on the steamboat Favorite, but could go no further by water than to within about three miles of Mankato, thence going on foot, arriving at their destination on the 5th of May.

Camp Pope was not an original settlement, but a spot selected especially as a base of operations against the Indians; for which purpose storehouses had been erected there. It was situated on the river about a mile and a quarter above the crossing of the Red Wood River. On the reassembling of the regiment the company held the same rank (5th) and position (7th) as before, but had as neighbours Company G on the right and Company I on the left.

In the latter part of the month (May) a regimental band was formed, and Seidel, Eberdt, and Jakobi were detailed as members of it. J. J. Mueller and Reimers rejoined on the 5th. Detert was detailed as regimental pioneer on the 15th. The expedition being ready, those sick and unable to travel were left behind at Camp Pope; of Company E, Hellmann and Paul Paulson remained there. The strength of the company present at this time was 68, and aggregate number 85.

The second expedition for the chastisement of the Dakotas left Camp Pope on the 16th of June, 1863. The 19th and 21st of the month were spent in camp. On the 23rd, transportation permitting,

71

the knapsacks of the men were carried in wagons. The valley between Big Stone Lake and Lake Traverse was reached on the 26th, and a camp established about a mile from the latter on the south side of the Minnesota River (there but a rivulet), which camp was situated near but outside of the state boundary. The camp was called McLaren, and three days were spent there.

From here a detachment consisting of three companies of infantry, including Company H of the Sixth Regiment, some cavalry, and one piece of artillery, all under command of Lieutenant Colonel Averill, was dispatched to Fort Abercrombie for supplies. Klinghammer, unable to march, was sent along to the fort. It may be here noted, as a matter of interest to hydrographers, that Lake Traverse was not at this time an unbroken sheet of water, as a corporal of Company G crossed it on foot near the middle, seeing the lake in two parts, to the right and left of him.

Resumed the march on June 30th, and forded the Sheyenne River on the 4th of July, camping a little beyond it at a spot three-quarters of a mile northeast of the two mounds called "The Bowshot" and in the neighbourhood of where the fight occurred about forty years before between the Pawnees, Shawnees, and Sheyennes, which, as I am informed, resulted in the annihilation of the last-named tribe. At this place,—named Camp Hayes,—70 miles distant from Camp McLaren, the expedition lay six days, awaiting the supply train, which arrived on the 9th. Resumed the march on the 11th, on which day Lieutenant Exel left on furlough. The 12th was spent in camp. The second crossing of the Sheyenne was made on the 17th.

On the 18th arrived at two lakes named Jessie [2] and Leda, 90 miles from Camp Hayes. An entrenched camp was established on the banks of the former (the more easterly one of these two lakes) which was about three miles long. The camp was called Atchison, and a day and one-half were spent there in making arrangements for a vigorous pursuit of the Indians. Companies C and G of the Sixth were stationed there as a part of the garrison, and five of the company were left behind there, *viz.*: Seidel, Eberdt, and Jakobi, as members of the band, and Kraemer and Reuter, who were too sick to travel.

On the 20th, all the arrangements having been completed, the

---

2. This camp was located on the W. 1/2 of the N.W. 1/4 of section 28, and the E. 1/2 of the N.E. 1/4 of section 29, township 147 north, of range 60 west, on the northeast side of what is now known as Lake Sibley, and about 11 miles in a direct line to the northwest of Cooperstown, Griggs County, North Dakota.—T. H. L.

expedition began a more rapid advance in pursuit of the enemy, and on the 24th of July, 89 miles from Camp Atchison was fought the battle of "Big Hills" or "Big Mound." As soon as it was known that the Indians were in force, the train was corralled on the margin of a small lake, Big Mound being directly to the eastward and distant about one and one-quarter miles. The Sixth Regiment with one company of Mounted Rangers and a section of artillery occupied the east front, and threw up a line of earthworks for protection.

As soon as the attack began, Colonel Crooks at once deployed Companies E, I, and K of the Sixth and A of the Ninth, under Major McLaren, as skirmishers, and they pursued the Indians two and one-half miles. Three companies of the Sixth were also deployed on the left flank, and the Indians were repulsed at that point. Major McLaren with companies A, B, D, I, and K advanced four miles at a double-quick, having been ordered to support the troops already at the front, but on their arrival they were ordered to return to camp.

On the 25th the expedition moved only about five miles to a better camping place and remained there on account of the jaded horses. On the 26th, with the Sixth Regiment in advance, the march was resumed. On arriving at Dead Buffalo Lake, some 15 miles from the last camp, the Indians again appeared in force and commenced an attack. Colonel Crooks immediately deployed a part of the Sixth, including Company E, as skirmishers, under Lieutenant Colonel Averill, and they advanced steadily, driving the enemy as they went; the remainder of the regiment under Major McLaren being held in reserve.

After an advance of about one and one-half miles Major McLaren with five companies of the Sixth was ordered to return to the camp at the lake, three companies remaining at the front. Desultory firing was kept up until about 3 p.m., when the Indians made a final assault, which was repulsed in fine style by the troops under command of Major McLaren. The Indians, having been defeated at every point, now withdrew from the field.

On the morning of the 27th the advance was again resumed, and in the afternoon a camp was formed on Stony Lake. On the 28th, as the troops were forming in column, the Indians again appeared and made their last charge. About one mile beyond the lake the Sixth Regiment was deployed to skirmish on the right of the train, and they repelled the attack of the Indians who threatened it. The firing continued for a time, the Indians finally making a rapid retreat in the face of the advancing expedition. The pursuit was continued until Apple

River was reached, where a camp was formed for the night.

On the 29th the army crossed Apple River, continuing the pursuit, and in the afternoon the Missouri River was reached, the regiment, under the immediate command of Colonel Crooks, skirmishing nearly two miles through the woods to it. The Indians having crossed to the west bank and hoisted white flags, the battery which had been advanced, and was in good position for shelling, was moved away, as the policy seemed to be to kill Indians only when they made an attack. Many of the skirmishers ventured to the river bank and began filling their canteens, when suddenly the enemy fired at them from the other side and the men were forced back, but not without sending a volley in return.

A camp was formed on the banks of the Missouri River near the mouth of Apple River. The point on the river struck was in about 46 deg. 40' north latitude, 600 miles from Fort Snelling by the route followed, 6 miles above the mouth of Apple River, and 85 miles from the Big Mound.

On the 30th Colonel Crooks with Companies A, I, and K and details of men from other regiments, proceeded to the Indian crossing, and destroyed all the wagons and such other property as would be of service to the Indians, and then returned to camp.

The return march began on the 2nd of August. The 5th and 9th of the month were spent in camp. Passed to the southward of the outward journey, shortening the route some thirty miles, and arrived at Camp Atchison on the 10th. Rested on the 11th. Reached Sheyenne River on the 13th, and camped three miles beyond it.

At this last place the nightly entrenching, commenced on departure from Camp Pope, was abandoned, the impulse of discontinuance coming from Company E. It had been the custom, both in the campaign of 1862 and this, to throw up every evening light exterior mounds and ditches for defence, a work necessarily irksome and unpopular with men fatigued with hard marching, and in the presence of an enemy (and sometimes not) they neither respected nor feared.

The traces of these works, slight as they were, will be visible for years, and if properly noted by the surveyors of the public lands as the surveys extend westward, and by future Pacific Railroad parties, will furnish means for exactly determining the routes of the two expeditions; certainly as regards that of 1863, which lay through trackless wastes, over which not even an odometer passed with this expedition. It is to be regretted that the commanding officer of the expedition,

74

lavish as were the expenses attending it, thought fit to negative a proposition made to form a quasi-topographical force for its use. Such a proposition would have involved no other expense than that of a few simple instruments for the use of the surveyor and his assistants (enlisted men) who might be detailed, and their labours would have furnished valuable material for the maps which were afterwards ordered to be constructed, besides contributing to the interests of geographical science in general.

The 16th and 18th of August were spent in camp. Reached Fort Abercrombie on the 21st and camped on the west side of it; distance from Camp Atchison about 115 miles. Remained at the fort three days. Here Klinghammer rejoined. Resumed march on the 25th. Spent the 30th in camp. Arrived at Sauk Centre on the 2nd of September, and remained there all the next day. Here Rehse was left behind, sick. At this place the expeditionary forces were divided, the Sixth Regiment being ordered to Fort Snelling. We left Sauk Centre on the 5th; and spent the next day in camp. The route was by the way of St. Joseph, St. Cloud, and Anoka, and the neighbourhood of the fort was reached on the 12th; the return route from Apple River being about 510 miles.

John and Scher rejoined on arrival at the fort, and Seidel, Eberdt, and Jakobi were relieved, the band being temporarily suspended. Corporal Eheim was sent to the hospital on the 18th.

Companies A, C, E, F, G, and H, being ordered to Fort Ridgley, left together on September 19th, going by the way of Bloomington, Shakopee, Jordan, Belle Plaine, and Le Sueur. At the latter place Gantner rejoined on the 22nd. Passed through Traverse, and came to Fort Ridgley on the 25th. Detert was now relieved. Here the destinations of the companies ordered to guard the southwestern frontier of the state were announced. Of Company E the main body (or two-thirds) was to proceed to the station at Lake Hanska in Brown county (35 miles off) and the remainder to the post of Cottonwood (12 miles), to relieve the troops there in garrison. Accordingly on the 28th the movement took place, the smaller force reaching its assigned position the same day, the main body taking two days for its journey. While at Lake Hanska, Sergeant Bell left for St. Paul, where, on the 9th of November, he was commissioned second lieutenant of the company.

Company E, having been designated (in lieu of Company F) as part of the escort to the train fitting out to convey provisions to the Indian bands removed from Minnesota to Crow Creek Agency or Fort Thompson on the Missouri River, was ordered to rendezvous at New Ulm, which was done on the 29th of October by both the detachments. The smaller one had left Big Cottonwood on the 25th under orders to garrison Buffalo Creek station (25 miles northeast of the fort), but immediately on reaching that place received the counter order. By the promotion of Sergeant Bell to the second lieutenancy, Sergeant Huhn became first or orderly sergeant, according to company order of the 1st of November.

Left New Ulm on the 3rd of the month, and reached Mankato, 28 miles distant, the assembling point of the train and escort, the next day. Eberdt and Jakobi left on the 4th to report at Fort Ridgley, and Lieutenant Holl for St. Paul. Seidel and Sproesser left, on the 6th, for Fort Ridgley, Corporal Steifel was sent there sick, and Radke was sent to the hospital at Mankato on the same day.

The expedition, with Captain J. C. Whitney in command, started on the 7th. The escort consisted of Companies D, E, and H, of the Sixth Regiment. The 9th, 10th, and 11th were spent in camp, also the 14th at Leavenworth, where the nuts were taken off the wagons (said to have been done by the men of Company D who felt themselves aggrieved). Sergeant Siebert, sick, left for St. Peter on the 15th, and Bast on furlough; from which, falling sick, he did not return at the appointed time. Reached Des Moines River, near the outlet of Lake Shetek, on the 18th, and there remained in camp all the next day. Here Lieutenant Holl rejoined and commenced to act as first lieutenant, having been commissioned as such November 7th; the present strength of the company was now 59, and aggregate 79. G. Paulson accompanied the expedition, but is not reckoned in this number, as he was on detached service at the headquarters of the expedition.

The route of the train was a few miles to the northward of the Red Pipe Stone Quarry, and the Big Sioux River was reached and crossed—53 miles from Lake Shetek—on the 23rd. Crossed the James River, 90 miles from the Big Sioux, on the 28th. Arrived at Fort Thompson, 75 miles further, on the 2nd of December, and remained there three days. This fort is a stockaded inclosure about 500 feet square, built to include and protect the Agency and barracks; it is 95 miles, by river road, above Fort Randall, two miles from the Missouri, and about a mile from Crow Creek.

On the 5th left the fort for return. Remained in camp on the 14th, twelve miles below Yankton; Corporal Leitner was promoted fifth sergeant, and privates Juergens, Gaheen, and Hoscheid appointed to fill the vacant offices of sixth, seventh, and eighth corporal. The 17th was also spent in camp on account of a terrible snowstorm. Reached the neighbourhood of Sioux City, Iowa, on the 18th, camping two and one-half miles northwest of it. On the 21st the troops again moved; travelling by the way of Melbourne, Cherokee, Peterson's, Spirit Lake, and Estherville, Iowa, they came to Fairmont, Minnesota, on the 30th. Remained in camp the next two days. Passed through Winnebago City and arrived at Mankato on the 3rd of January, 1864, when Company D left for the north.

This journey of about 750 miles—315 outward from, and 435 return to, Mankato—was accomplished in fifty-four days; and because of the rigor of the Northwestern winter, and much of it through a pathless country,—the command sleeping in tents on the snow-covered ground,—the men called it the "Moscow journey." The mercury at times stood 30 deg. below zero, and never was above the freezing point.

Companies E and H returned by way of New Ulm to Fort Ridgley, 45 miles, on the 7th and 8th of January, having marched since leaving the former place in November about 825 miles. The only company of the Sixth Regiment at the fort at this time was A. Company E was assigned quarters in the stone barracks, on north side. The duties were not heavy and the time passed comfortably enough for soldiers. Musicians Seidel, Eberdt, Jakobi, and Sproesser now rejoined, but not for duty, being detailed in the band; also Sergeant Steifel and George Paulson. Sergeant Siebert rejoined on the 20th. Sergeant Huhn was detached as acting post hospital steward on the 27th, being afterwards discharged—on the 20th of February—to enlist in the same capacity in the regular army. Henry Steck, enlisted as private in the regiment on the 3rd of February and assigned to the company, joined for duty March 20th,—native country of recruit, Wurtemberg.

Bast rejoined on the 10th, and Radke about the 15th. Captain Schoenemann left for St. Paul April 4th, and Lieutenant Holl assumed command of the company. On the 19th Sergeant Siebert was promoted to first sergeant and Corporal Stiefel to fifth sergeant, and privates Radke and Gabbert appointed seventh and eighth corporals, respectively; but the latter scarcely ever acted as such and was reduced to the ranks, at his own request, on the 13th of the following month. George Paulson was detailed in the regimental band on the 7th of May.

At the beginning of May a detail of about a dozen men of the company, under Sergeant Huth and Corporal Radke, were sent from Fort Ridgley to Milford—twelve miles—to relieve the cavalry at that post. On the 15th Corporal Smith replaced Corporal Radke there. This detachment returned at the end of the month. While there the woods of the Big Cottonwood and in the neighbourhood of Milford were thoroughly scouted, both by parties from Company E and from Company G (posted at Fort Wilkin and Madelia), but by the former traces only of the Indians were found.

The Sixth Regiment being ordered to rendezvous at Fort Snelling, to prepare for their departure to the South, in accordance with the order of the War Department of the 26th of May requiring it to report at Helena, Arkansas, Companies A, E, and H left Fort Ridgley on the 2nd of June. The only member of the company left behind there was F. Henricks, sick in hospital. Traveled by the way of Henderson, Belle Plaine, and Shakopee, and arrived at Fort Snelling on the 7th, and went into camp about a mile above the fort—Camp Crooks.

Between the 8th and 12th the following recruits joined the company for duty as privates, *viz.*: Edward Bryan, a native of Ireland, enlisted November 7th, 1863; Henry Wetterau, native of Wisconsin, enlisted February 4th, 1864; Peter Holtzmer, native of Luxemburg, enlisted February 5th; Joseph Rachel, enlisted February 11th; Michael Knopf, native of New York, enlisted February 24th; Charles Foglesang, native of Baden, and William Hildebrandt, native of Hanover, enlisted February 26th; Mathias Frank, native of Luxemburg, enlisted February 27th; Stephen Iwan, and Francz Troska, natives of Prussian Poland, enlisted February 29th; John Lieber, native of Nassau, enlisted June 10th,—and all were enlisted for three years.

Of these Bryan had been enlisted for the company at St. Paul, but having been at once placed on detached service did not join his command till this time (the 8th); with him, from the same duty—herding mules at Glencoe—returned Rehse. Corporal Gaheen was detailed in the regimental colour guard on the 12th; and on the 14th Captain Schoenemann resumed command, and Burch rejoined.

The sum of the distance travelled by the company from its organization to this time was over 2,700 miles.

PART 4

Services at Helena, St. Louis, and New Orleans—1864-65

On the 14th of June, 1864, the whole regiment left Fort Snelling, marched to St. Paul, and embarked on the steamboats *Enterprise* and *Hudson*, each having two barges in tow for additional accommodation of the men. Arrived at Dunleith, Illinois, on the 17th and took the cars to Cairo, which point was reached on the 19th. Here wagoner Henricks, sick, was left in the hospital. Embarked on the steamer *Empress* at midnight, and arrived at Helena, Arkansas, and landed there, on the 23rd.

By changes in commissions occurring during the spring, the company had now become the third in rank and in regimental position the fifth from the right, with Company A in front and Company I in the rear or left. Its strength at the time of the arrival was, present 76, aggregate 84; the absentees being Lieutenant Bell and A. J. Hill on detached service, the two Henricks and Schauer sick, and Scheer, Iwan, and Troska left behind at St. Paul.

The regiment at once went into camp, on the bank of the river, one-half mile above the town. Shelter tents were issued now for the first time. The camp was called Camp Buford, and was the last one that was officially named. Troska and Iwan rejoined on the 24th, and also the next day A. J. Hill from detached service at Washington. Detert and Scheibel were detailed as regimental pioneers on the 28th and A. J. Hill as company clerk in the beginning of July.

From the beginning there was a close guard kept around the limited area occupied by the regiment, and it was maintained several weeks. The duty required by the District Commandant was chiefly prison and picket guard. In the first week of July orders were issued to build quarters, and fatigue parties were at once set to work cutting, hauling, and sawing logs for that purpose. Wagoner Henricks rejoined on the 18th.

Companies E and F being detailed to proceed to certain points with a view of obtaining information of the movements of the enemy, the major part embarked, with forty men of the Fifteenth Illinois Cavalry, on the evening of the 13th, on the steamboat *Dove*, and proceeded up the Mississippi River, reaching Buck Island (No. 52) on the next day, and searched it as ordered. Returned to the levee at Helena the same night, and lay there. Next day, the 15th, went up the St. Francis River, some thirty-five miles, to Alligator Bayou, then returned to Helena and into camp again. The Mississippi River part of this trip was under command of Captain Schoenemann, and the other under that of the major of cavalry. No guerrillas or other enemies were seen. The infantry forces did not land, but the cavalry did and scouted between the two rivers.

Kilian was detached as nurse in the regimental hospital on the 21st. Lieutenant Bell returned on the 22nd, and with him Scheer.

On the 26th of July the regiment went out about two miles beyond the picket lines on the Little Rock road to cover the retreat of some coloured troops and cavalry who had been very severely handled that morning at a creek some few miles west of town. On the 1st of August it went out again on the same road as before, but not quite so far, and remained on picket in the woods on the right of the road during the night, returning to camp the next morning. It was understood that a projected attack by the enemy on the defences of the town was the cause of this movement. Nothing of the kind, however, took place.

The heat was now intense, and the sickness increased with alarming rapidity. The building of quarters was given up or postponed, and the houses, more or less finished, occupied as well as they could be. Company E managed to complete—walls and roof—one of the four prescribed barracks, but, being destitute of chinking, in a rainstorm it afforded but poor shelter. Being composed of log and frame houses, board and canvas shanties, the camp of the Sixth Regiment presented, by autumn, a melancholy variety indeed.

Bast was detached for provost duty in Helena on the 16th; on the 18th Schafer was detached for provost duty, and Praxl as nurse in the post hospital on the 19th. J. J. Mueller was detached as cook in the regimental hospital (now in town) on the 20th.

The following men of the company died while at Helena, *viz.*:

Jean Rossion on July 25th; Joseph Rachel, July 27th; Louis Wetterau, August 5th; Frederick Schoenheiter on the 10th, Michael Boos on the 18th; August Willialms on the 23rd, and Henry Reuter on the 25th. The latter was the last of the company that died at Helena; all seven dying of disease. They were buried with the rest of the regimental dead on the summit of a rising ground about one-half mile northwest of the camp. Properly marked boards were placed at their graves.

In September the sick men had become so numerous that large numbers were sent north. Of Company E there went as follows: On the 1st of the month, Bristle was sent to the hospital at Memphis; Corporal Hoscheid, wagoner Henricks, Foglesang, Metz, Mueckenhausen, Rehse, Thiele, and H. Wetterau, sick, were sent to the hospital at Jefferson Barracks, Mo., on the 3rd; Sergeants Leitner and Stiefel, Corporals Neierburg, Juergens, and Radke, and Ferlein, Gabbert, Hauck, Holtzmer, John, Kilian, Kraemer, Krueger, M. Mueller, Munson, Schene, Steck, and Temme, sick, were also sent to Jefferson Barracks hospital, on the 19th. F. Henricks rejoined on the 21st, and on the same day Sergeant Rohde was relieved.

At about this time the once strong Sixth Regiment had become the shadow of its former self, and added little to the effective strength of the garrison of the post. It was pitiable to look at the companies as they marched to dress parade; very often having but half a dozen men in line.

Gantner was relieved on the 28th; and Bast rejoined on the 1st of October. The same day the following recruits, who had enlisted as privates for one year in the regiment, joined the company, and were two days afterwards assigned to it by regimental order, viz.: William S. Adams, native of Minnesota, enlisted August 25th; Henry Churchill, native of Vermont, enlisted August 27th; George R. Bell, native of Ohio, and Nelson A. Chandler, a native of New York, enlisted September 10th; Melchior Steinmann, a native of Switzerland, enlisted September 12th. All of the above but Adams (a Sioux of mixed blood) were young boys, and incapable of full military duty.

On the 12th, details of men commenced to build barracks on selected regimental grounds located in town, opposite to the church used as a Soldiers' Home. No order had been received to go into regular winter quarters, but the necessities of the case required this course. George Bell was detailed as orderly at regimental headquarters on the 21st. Sergeant Stiefel, and Foglesang and Schene rejoined on the 22nd.

The removal of the company to the log quarters on the east side of the above-named ground took place on the 25th. Company E was now shifted to the extreme left of the regiment, becoming the tenth from the right wing and the second in rank. Company I was on the immediate right of it.

An order from New Orleans requiring the regiment to report at St. Louis was received and read on the 3rd of November and preparations made at once to comply with the same. Detert, Scheibel, Kernen, and J. J. Mueller were relieved the same day and Schafer rejoined; also Burch and Praxl (the latter rejoined on the 2nd) were detached for provost duty in Helena. The two latter, with Churchill, sick, were all of the company left behind there.

On the 4th, the Twenty-Third Wisconsin having arrived to relieve it, the Sixth Minnesota embarked on the steamboat *Thomas E. Tutt*, truly glad to leave a place so associated with disease, suffering, and death. The number of the company now on the boat was 54, out of an aggregate of 80. While lying at Memphis, on the 6th, Bristle, wagoner Henricks, and Ferlein rejoined.

Arrived at St. Louis on the evening of the 11th, after a tedious voyage. Next morning the regiment disembarked and marched through the city. Six companies were quartered at Winter Street Barracks, E being among them. At this time the military post of St. Louis was under the enlightened command of Colonel James H. Baker of the Tenth Minnesota, whose regulations for the government of troops stationed there were liberal and just, and an admirable model for the imitation of officers having volunteer soldiers of the Republic under their control. The sojourn in this city would have been generally very pleasant had it not been for the incessant duty, which, consisting almost exclusively of prison guard, was severe, just half of the men's time being taken up by it. The weather, too, was very cold for outside posts of sentinels.

J. J. Mueller was detailed as orderly at company headquarters on the 12th, Kernen detached as cook in the regimental hospital on the 15th, and Steinmann detailed as company drummer on the 22nd. The absent members now began rapidly to return. M. Mueckenhausen rejoined on the 17th. Sergeant Leitner on the 21st, Burch, Praxl, Corporal Radke, and Kilian, Kraemer, and Temme on the 25th, Churchill on the 26th, M. Mueller on the 27th, and Krueger on the 30th. Eberdt was relieved on the 29th. Lieutenant Bell was dismissed from service by order of the Department Commander on the 29th. Knopf left on furlough December 9th, but sickness prevented him from returning at its expiration.

The companies in Winter Street Barracks moved into Schofield Barracks No. 2 on the 13th of December; E being quartered in the northern quadrangle. Corporal Gaheen was relieved on the 19th, and Sergeant Leitner detached as keeper at Gratiot Street Military Prison on the 20th. Metz rejoined on the 27th, and Holtzmer on the 29th. Lieutenant Bell, having been restored to command by order of the President of January 3rd, 1865, rejoined on the 10th. Kernen rejoined on the 11th. To fill vacancies occasioned by the death of Neierburg and reduction of Gabbert, Bast and Beckendorf were appointed seventh and eighth corporals on the 12th, and confirmed as such on the 17th.

Having been ordered to report at New Orleans, La., the regiment left St. Louis on the 29th of January, and travelled by rail to Cairo, where it was put on board the steamboat *W. R. Arthur*, which left the next evening. The boat then had on board over 1,000 souls in all. Reached New Orleans the 6th of February, and marched to quarters in Louisiana Cotton Press No. 1, used as a camp of distribution. Lieutenant Holl was detailed as assistant regimental quartermaster, and Corporal Gaheen again on colour guard, on the 7th.

The northern soldiers found much to amuse and instruct them when they arrived at this southwestern satrapy, for such—from its isolated position, its semi-tropical products, its swarthy and varied population, strange tongues, manners, and customs, and from its form of government—the Military Division of West Mississippi might well be termed. They, however, soon discovered the difference between New Orleans and St. Louis. The former was under the strictest rule of a martinet of the regular army. The accidental absence of a pass, even in daytime, or the slightest divergence from the prescribed dress, whether occurring on or off duty, rendered enlisted men subject to ruthless fine or imprisonment, and the other offending articles to confiscation by the provost marshal.

No duty was called for till the 10th, when, for two days, fatigue parties were set to work on the military railroad on St. Joseph street. On the 13th details for miscellaneous guard duty were furnished. Corporal Hoscheid and John rejoined on the 12th. Musician Chandler was transferred to Company B on the 13th, there being more than the regular number of musicians in Company E. Wagoner Henricks was detailed in regimental quartermaster's depot on the 15th. On the 19th the regiment moved into the barracks formerly Terrill's Cotton Press, opposite the southeast corner of Annunciation Square, just vacated by the Seventh Vermont. Sergeant Rohde was detailed as sergeant of police on the 20th. Eberdt and Gropel were detached to guard stores on steamboats, under command of an ordnance officer, on the 25th. Stengelin, sick, was sent to the general hospital on the 26th.

Towards the end of the month the regiment received orders to repair to Chalmette, and to report to the Sixteenth Army Corps, to which it had been assigned, as soon as relieved by a certain coloured regiment. On the 3rd of March, having been relieved, the regiment moved into the square immediately opposite, where, having a few days previously been supplied with shelter tents, a camp was established. J. J. Mueller was relieved on the 4th. The strength of the company was now as follows: Present, 66; absent, 11,—aggregate 77.

By this time it was authoritatively known that the Sixth Regiment belonged to the Second Brigade of the Second Division, Sixteenth Army Corps, Major General A. J. Smith commanding.

PART 5.

Services in Alabama; and Conclusion—1865

The regiment left New Orleans on the 6th of March and proceeded along the river six miles to the plain of Chalmette, where at a point a little below the old battlefield, and exactly opposite the present rebel earthworks, it embarked on the small ocean steamship *Cromwell*. Lieutenant Holl and wagoner Henricks did not go along with the company. This was a wretched voyage. The men were packed as closely as negroes on a slave-ship; the majority being unable to get more than sitting room, and no chance to lie at full length for sleep. In the afternoon of the 8th the troops were landed at Fort Gaines, Alabama, whence they marched to a camping ground on the south shore of the island (Dauphin) about two miles west of the fort.

Mahle was detached to serve on brigade provost guard by order issued on the 10th; Knopf and Stengelin rejoined on the 13th; and Scheibel was detached to serve in the Division Pioneer Company, by order issued on the 17th.

While at Dauphin Island the system of company cooking was abandoned, and that of distributing to each man his proportion of the rations, for disposal at will, adopted instead. Company cooks, consequently, were no longer required.

Broke camp on the 19th, and embarked at Fort Gaines on a gunboat (tin clad). Lay all night in Navy Cove near Fort Morgan. Next day the fleet crossed to Fish River and ascended it several miles to Dalney's Mill Landing, on the west side, where the force disembarked and went into camp, the Second Brigade being about a mile from the river on the south side of a small but rapid creek. While at this place breastworks were commenced to the west, but soon discontinued. Lieutenant Holl and wagoner Henricks rejoined on the 21st, the former having been relieved by the return of the regimental quarter-master.

On the 25th the forward march of the troops began, and eight miles were made. The next day the Second Brigade was in front and the Sixth Minnesota was detailed for skirmishing, Company E being employed to cover the left flank of the brigade while marching. The enemy's skirmishers hovered in front the whole time and an incessant fusillade was kept up. By noon the creek on which Cyrus Sibley's house and mills were was reached and crossed, and at about a mile beyond the company was halted, and remained, with some other companies, on picket there the whole night. The enemy's pickets and ours were often in view of each other and exchanged many shots. Next morning, the 27th, the rest of the regiment moved up and camped there; and breastworks were thrown up and a battery stationed on the right flank. On the 28th the regiment fell back; to the south side of the creek, where the camp of the Second Division was entrenched, immediately opposite Sibley's house.

Here there was very little to do or see, but time enough to listen to the almost continuous cannonading at the Spanish Fort, which however soon ceased to be an object of remark except when, occasionally, the rush of the enormous shells from the rebel gunboats drew every one's attention. A reconnoissance on the Blakely road, to a point three miles out, was made on the 2nd of April by the brigade. Near the place of return two torpedoes were exploded by the feet of the horses at the head of the column. On the same day Klinghammer, who had been arrested on Dauphin Island, for very insubordinate conduct, and subsequently tried by court-martial, found guilty, and sentenced to one year's hard labour at a military prison, was turned over to the provost marshal, and the company saw him no more.

On the 3rd the division broke camp and moved, by the way of Origen Sibley's mills, to the front, near Blakely, on the Tensas River, about twelve miles from Mobile, taking position on the left of the Thirteenth Corps, which had appeared before the enemy's defences there a few days previously.

About a mile and a half to the eastward of the rebel works immediately defending the town are some private graves among the pine trees, apparently the commencement of a cemetery, but without fencing or other general improvements. The tomb of one of General Marion's men, Godbold, is there; and, immediately to the north of it a couple of rods, a local family, the Wilkinsons, have a little plot of land, about fifteen paces square, surrounded by a low brick wall.

Here, shortly before sunset on the 3rd of April, the brigade encamped, the Sixth Minnesota being a couple of hundred paces distant from the brick graveyard, to the east and southeast of it. The troops were told to pitch no tents, light no fires, but lie on their arms, keep as quiet as possible, and await further orders. It was rumoured that the enemy's works were to be stormed that night, but we were not disturbed. The musicians, however, were called out and held subject to the surgeon's orders. Next day, the 4th, tents were pitched and the usual camp arrangements recommenced, except that all calls were discontinued lest the sound of the bugles and drums should reach the enemy's ears and guide them in shelling our camp.

While here a large detail was furnished every day by the regiment for duty in the trenches and on the skirmish line. Before sunrise each morning the soldiers filed off through the gloomy ravines to their posts in the trenches and pits of the advance, some half a mile away, there to lie and exchange shots with the enemy, and subject to their shells, till relieved. Fortunately during the week spent in this camp not a man of the company was injured, and it is understood that but two casualties (slight wounds) occurred in the regiment the whole time the siege of Blakely lasted. On two or three occasions shells reached the brigade camp, one of which cut off a thick pine near to Godbold's grave, but did not injure either living or dead. These shots were provoked by men climbing the tall pine trees to get sight of the enemy's works. The bombardment of the Spanish Fort on the evening of the 8th was very plainly heard. It lasted from 5:30 o'clock to 7, and the reports averaged about thirty a minute, by count.

In the afternoon of the next day tents were struck and the regiment left camp, knapsacks packed, at 4 o'clock, and moved silently through the woods to the line of trenches used by the reserve of the picket guard, and there, knapsacks being unslung and with other impediments piled together, the men were stationed to await orders. Immediately to the right of the Sixth was a battery and beyond that another regiment, also posted in reserve; and on the left there was nothing. From this position to the enemy's redoubts it was about half a mile in a direct course westward, and from the advanced skirmish line to the same works some 400 yards.

About 5:15 p.m. the various batteries of the Union forces opened fire upon the enemy's lines, but their guns did not reply for about ten minutes, when the cannonading became brisk on both sides, lasting until 25 minutes to 6; the battery near the regiment sharing in it. Now it ceased suddenly on our side, and in its place were heard the ringing cheers of the soldiers as they rose, in full view of the reserves, from their trenches in the front and rushed towards the Confederate fortifications. By 6 o'clock the noise of the cannon had ceased and a white flag was visible, which told of the enemy's surrender; and shortly the Stars and Stripes superseded it. Thus, on the evening of the 9th of April, 1865, took place the battle of Blakely, which, like that of New Orleans in 1815, was fought after the necessity for it had passed away.

The regiment returned to the original camp for the night. Next morning if crossed the battle grounds and encamped immediately within the former hostile earthworks, about a quarter of a mile from the village, but remained there only two days, returning on the 12th to the neighbourhood of the cemetery. Here Ferlein, unable to march, was left behind.

Without the men having any idea as to where they were going, the line of march was taken up on the morning of the 13th of April, but a few hours proved that it was neither to Mobile nor to Pensacola, but to the north, showing that the Sixteenth Corps was on one of its characteristic marches again. The strength of the company was now: Present, 63; aggregate, 76. For over sixty miles the route lay through pine forests, with very few clearings; and the villages then successively passed were Burnt Corn, Midway, Activity, Greenville, and Sandy Ridge. No enemy was seen, but, on the contrary, when the settled country was reached, every house displayed a white flag or cloth, generally with the words "The Union Forever" on it.

On the 19th, a few miles south of Midway, the official news of the surrender of Lee's army overtook the expedition; and at camp on the 24th the rumour of Mr. Lincoln's death, not at first believed, met it. For thirteen days, to the 25th, the troops marched each day, arriving then at a stream five miles south of Montgomery, having travelled a distance of 170 miles, from the cemetery near Blakely. The 26th was spent in camp, to rest and wash. On the 27th the troops moved through the city,—the cradle of the rebel government,—and encamped beyond it. The camp of the brigade was just beyond a swamp on the river road, about two miles northeastward of the city. From the 26th to the 30th, as the transports had not arrived, the soldiers were supplied by foraging parties with cornmeal, supplies of fresh beef, and a little bacon. F. Henricks and Knopf, sick, were sent to the hospital in the city, May

2nd. Ferlein rejoined on the 8th.

On the 18th of May the regimental camp was moved about a mile further from the river, nearly to the Wetumka road, to get higher ground and purer water. Sergeant Leitner rejoined on the 22nd. Lieutenant Holl left on sick furlough on the 25th. Eberdt and Gropel rejoined on the 26th, the former being detailed in the band on the 29th. On the 31st Sergeant Steifel was honorably discharged for disability contracted while in the service. The same day a review of the Second Division took place. Private Ferlein was honourably discharged on the 1st of June, his term of service having expired.

On the same day Mahle and Scheibel rejoined, and Huth was sent to the hospital. On the 6th soft bread was issued for the first time in three months. Jakobi was sent to the hospital in town on the 13th. Sergeant Huth (in hospital) and privates Gantner and Parks were honourably discharged on the 15th, their terms of service having expired. On the 25th Krueger was sent to the division hospital in town. The same day Schermann died of disease. He was buried near the second mile-post on the Wetumka road. On the 30th Corporals Sauer and Joseph Smith were promoted fourth and fifth sergeants, respectively, and J. Mueller and Blesius seventh and eighth corporals,—to take effect on the 16th of June. Knopf rejoined July 1st. Private Jakobi was honorably discharged on the 7th for disability contracted while in the service; and on the same day the regiment acted as guard at a military execution. Private Schene died of disease on the 8th, and was buried in the city cemetery. Musician Seidel was honourably discharged on the 9th, his term of service having expired. He was the last man discharged previous to the general mustering out.

On the 13th the men whose terms of service did not expire before the 1st of October were transferred to and ordered to join the Fifth Regiment; those from Company E being as follows: Bryan, Foglesang, Frank, Hildebrandt, Holtzmer, Iwan, Knopf, Lieber, and Troska. While at Montgomery, by change of captains in Company D, Company E became the first in rank, its appropriate position in regimental line being the first on the right flank, with Company I on the left.

After much weary waiting the regiment at last received orders to proceed to Vicksburg, to be mustered out, and, joyfully striking tents for the last time, on the 16th embarked on the steamer *Coquette* for Selma, which place was reached next morning. Here, instead of proceeding at once, the regiment remained three days by reason of change of opinions in regard to the recruits just transferred. The order transferring them was revoked, and they were returned to their companies to be mustered out with the main body. The strength of Company E was now as follows: Present, 60; absent, 6,—aggregate, 62.

On the 20th, left Selma by railroad. Reached Demopolis in the afternoon, and descended the river there, on a steamboat, four miles to the continuation of the railroad on the west bank, which place was known as McDowell's Landing. Here camped for the night. The next day arrived at Meridian, Mississippi, and lay there over night, and on the day after, the 22nd, arrived at Pearl River opposite Jackson. Owing to the destruction of the bridge over this stream, and that of the Big Black, there was a gap of over thirty miles in the railroad communication, which had to be traversed the best way possible. Most of the men walked, having hired teams for their things. By the 25th nearly all of the regiment had rendezvoused on the west side of the Big Black River, near the railroad. The next day took cars for Vicksburg.

The regiment was now, it seems, ordered to report at St. Louis, and accordingly, on the evening of the 26th, embarked at Vicksburg on the steamboat *Missouri* for that place. Having arrived at St. Louis on the 31st, it received orders to proceed to Fort Snelling, and on the 1st of August started on the steamboat *Brilliant* for St. Paul. Private W. Smith was found dead in his place on the deck on the morning of August 3rd, and his body was left at Burlington, Iowa, for interment. On the 7th arrived at St. Paul, where a most cordial reception by the citizens was experienced, and after being entertained at the capitol, re-embarked and went to Fort Snelling. Here Lieutenant Holl, and F. Henricks, Krueger, Schauer, Simon, and some others who had remained at Jackson, rejoined.

The company was mustered out, with the rest of the regiment, on the 19th of August, at the fort. Of the original members there were now discharged 47, who had served their full three years. Their names were as follows, *viz.*: Bast, Beckendorf, J. B. Bell, Besecke, Blesius, Blessner, Bristle, Burch, Detert, Eberdt, Gaheen, Goldner, Gropel, Hahn, F. Henricks, H. Henricks, A. J. Hill, Holl; Hoscheid, John, Kernen, Kilian, Kraemer, Krueger, Leitner; Mahle; Martin, Metz, M. Mueckenhausen, J. J. Mueller, M. Mueller, G. Paulson, Praxl, Radke, Reimers, Rohde, Sauer, Schafer, Scheer, Scheibel, Schoenemann, Siebert, Simon, J. Smith, Sproesser, Stengelin, and Temme, The recruits discharged numbered 12, and were: G. Bell, Bryan, Churchill, Foglesang, Frank, Hildebrandt, Holtzmer, Iwan, Knopf, Lieber, Steinmann, and Troska.

Although the foregoing pages are but a history of one company of the Sixth Regiment, yet in general the account of its movements applies generally to all.

The lot of this regiment, as an organization, was somewhat peculiar, and, in respect to military glory, unfortunate. It boasts of no hard won victories, laments no disheartening defeats, but it did faithfully its assigned duty; and, in so doing, deserved well of the Republic.

PART 6

Tables and Statistics

COMPOSITION OF ORIGINAL COMPANY

Nationality: 82 men were of German blood, 4 born in North America; 4 of American (U.S.); 4 of Scandinavian; 2 of French; 1 of Magyar; and 1 of British.

Religions: Proportion of Lutheran and Methodist, 25 *per cent.*; Roman Catholic, 19 *per cent.*; Rationalistic, 17 *per cent.*; and 39 *per cent.* were unclassified.

Occupations: Proportion of farmers, 30 *per cent.*; mechanics, 54 *per cent.*; professional men, 8 *per cent.*; and miscellaneous and unknown, 8 *per cent.*

STATISTICS OF DISEASE.

Previous to the summer of 1864 the health of the regiment had always been very good. At the time of the departure for the South the proportion of sick in the whole company was under 5 per cent., the cases being mostly of a trivial nature. The following table, compiled from the monthly returns, will show how rapidly the ratio increased during the sojourn at Helena:

Day.	Whole Number of Sick.	Aggregate of Company	Percentage of Sick.
June 30	10	84	12
July 31	24	82	30
August 31	41	78	52
September 30	46	76	60
October 31	30	81	37

The "daily" and "extra" duty men would swell the last column somewhat if their health had been generally reported, but it is not customary to enter their names in the "sick" book. Every man of the company was sick at one time or another while in the South.

The poor economy of sending the regiment to Helena immediately from a northern climate at the commencement of the summer, and keeping it there so long, is plainly seen in the following calculation (and other companies showed a similar state of things to Company E): If we take the sum of the "aggregates" of the morning reports during each month the product is the maximum number of days' service the government can expect for that period, but which, however, it really never gets. By similarly adding together the columns of "sick" we have a figure representing loss of service, and which should be within reasonable limits.

While in Minnesota this loss never amounted to 20 *per cent.* of the whole service due, and generally fluctuated between 8 and 17. In a space of time equal to and immediately preceding the time spent at Helena,—nineteen weeks,—it was as low as 3 *per cent.*; while there it was 43; and for the same length of time immediately after leaving Helena, it was 23. In March, 1865, it was 13; in April, 13; in May, 18; and in June, 27. As no morning reports were made after the middle of July, the figures for the remainder of the term of service cannot be obtained, but undoubtedly they would result in at least 30 *per cent.*

The number of deaths occurring while in Helena, and traceable to disease contracted while at that point and Montgomery, is 13, equal to 15 *per cent.*, or nearly one-sixth of the whole company.

NUMERICAL SUMMARIES.

Members.

Resigned, 1; transferred, 13; discharged previous to expiration of service, 16; died, 14; deserted, 2; missing, 1; mustered out at expiration of service in June and July, 1865, 5; mustered out *in corpore* August 19th, 1865, 59; in military prison and unknown, 2. Total number of members, 113.

Occupation of Time.

En route, on campaigns and expeditions, 177 days. *En route*, changing stations, 68 days. Stationary, at posts and barracks, 439 days. Stationary in camp, 412 days. Total, or entire term of service, 3 years.

Distances Travelled, Approximately.

On foot, 2,800 miles; in wagons, 100 miles; by steamboat, 4,235 miles; by railroad, 865 miles. Total, 8,000 miles.

Limits and Extent of Country Traversed.

Latitude: From 47 deg. 32', at Lake Jessie, D. T., approximate position, to 27 deg., at the mouth of the Mississippi; being 20 deg. 32' difference, equal to 1,416 statute miles, measured on a meridian line.

Longitude: From 86 deg. 25', at Montgomery, Ala., to 100 deg. 35', at the mouth of Apple River, D. T., approximate position; being 14 deg. 10' difference, equal to 757 statute miles on the line of middle latitude.

Greatest included right line: From Lake Jessie, D. T., approximate position, to the mouth of the Mississippi; course S. 21 deg. E., distance 1,372 miles.

An air line drawn from Montgomery, Alabama, the last station, to St. Paul, Minnesota, would be 945 miles in length, course N.N.W. The water route to the latter place, *via* Mississippi Sound and New Orleans, is about 2,350 miles; while that actually travelled, *via* Vicksburg, is about 1,585 miles.

Appendix

LIEUT. COL. MARSHALL'S RAID INTO DAKOTA—1862.[1]

BY

CAPT. CHARLES J. STEES.

After the memorable release of the captives at Camp Release, the scouts were very diligent in searching out and locating the numerous small bands of hostile Indians who were scattered through the country to the north and west of the camp. Upon learning that there were several lodges of Indians to the westward in the vicinity of Wild Goose Nest Lake, General Sibley, under date of October 13th, 1862, directed Lieutenant Colonel Marshall of the Seventh Regiment to take command of an expedition detailed to capture any bands to be found along the upper Lac qui Parle valley, and, if necessary, to go as far as the western side of the Coteaus, about 45 miles distant.

October 13th (1862). Cold, windy day. Company G was ordered to be ready to move at 12 o'clock, midnight, with six days' rations. The men thought they were going below with the prisoners, but were disappointed on learning that we were off on an Indian hunt. The expedition under Lieutenant Colonel Marshall consisted of Company G, of the Sixth Regiment, under command of Captain Valentine; 100 men of the Third Regiment—50 mounted—under Lieutenant Swan; Company B, Seventh Regiment, Captain Curtis; a mountain howitzer with 8 men under Sergeant O'Shea; Major Joseph R. Brown and 4 scouts (Bell, Quinn, and two Indians). Left Camp Release at 10 p.m. for the Lac qui Parle valley. It was very cold travelling, so much so that

---

1. From the journal of Charles J. Stees, late captain of Company G, Sixth Regiment, Minnesota Volunteer Infantry, and formerly major of the Fourth Regiment, Third Brigade, First Division, Pennsylvania Infantry.

the water froze in our canteens.

October 14th. We made a very rapid march during the night, and reached the Lac qui Parle River before daybreak, made a bridge, using the wagons for the purpose, and all crossed over. Soon after passed a deserted bark village. The scouts reported that there were Indians ahead with eight ox teams, but there was nothing to be seen but the sky and prairie. The Indians, discovering that they were pursued, now fired the prairie in front of us with the evident intention of retarding our movements and to prevent our horses from having forage. The wind being high, it carried the burnt dirt and ashes along in clouds, flying into our eyes, and they became very painful and bloodshot. Was appointed officer of the guard for the night, and, by using three reliefs of 15 men each, dug six rifle-pits for the protection of the camp.

October 15th. Aroused the camp at 4 o'clock, struck the tents, and was on the march by 6 a.m. Following up the Lac qui Parle, at 10 o'clock we captured four prisoners,—an Indian warrior, a half-breed boy, and two squaws. The half-breed was a son of Roubillard, a Frenchman who lived back of us in St. Paul, in 1851. I used to play with him. He speaks French, English, and Sioux, and gave us much information about what we were after. A short distance beyond we crossed the state line into Dakota Territory. William Wallace, E. J. Van Slyke, and I visited one of the line posts, which was marked, "26 miles from Big Stone Lake" (located about eight miles north of Gary, South Dakota); and the other three sides were marked "Minnesota," "Dakota," and "1859." Wallace was on the survey and helped plant the post. In order to celebrate the event, each of us, with one foot in Dakota and the other in Minnesota, shook hands together.

We were now in sight of Re Wakan or Spirits Hill (so named by the Dakotas). Although distant, the appearance of the Coteau des Prairies, as they loom up like a dark wall against the clear western sky, is very beautiful. Halted in a hollow for a lunch. The scouts returned and reported 19 Indian lodges ahead, which made the men feel joyful at the prospect of a fight. Marched three miles further and camped for the night in a beautiful dell at the headwaters of the Lac qui Parle. One wagon and six Indians were brought in. Of those captured up to this time, the young men were held as prisoners, and the squaws and children were given into the custody of the old men and ordered to report at Camp Release, and they faithfully followed the instructions.

October 16th. During the night wolves were howling in the vicinity of the camp. Left camp before daylight and commenced ascending the Coteau des Prairies, the highest table-land in this section of the United States, and full of lakes. A chain of twenty or more lakes could be seen from the highest point, which form the headwaters of the Lac qui Parle, Yellow Medicine, and Whetstone Rivers, on one side, and furnish many tributary streams to the Big Sioux on the west side,— many miles of land and bluffs, prairies, and lakes seeming as not ten miles distant.

At various points we passed through fields of buffalo bones. Arrived at "Two Lakes" (Mde-nonpana), where the Indians camped last night and left a sign indicating that they had moved to the westward two days previously. In order to overtake them, Colonel Marshall took the mounted men, howitzer, and the best teams, and pushed ahead, leaving the infantry and baggage train, under command of Captain Valentine, to follow on his trail and camp at the next creek for the night, with instructions to continue the forward movement if he did not return. Instead of following instructions, Captain Valentine crossed the creek, and, ascending the next hill, perceived what appeared to be a beautiful lake a few miles distant; he continued the march, intending to camp there; so we marched and marched, but no lake appeared; the men, worn and fatigued, lagged behind, some straggling back for five miles, and curses, loud and deep, were heard on every hand,—the lake turned out to be a mirage, a sight not uncommon in this region. Failing to arrive at the lake, we finally camped in the prairie grass, without wood or water; and, the rations being short, we went to sleep, supperless, after marching until 10 o'clock at night.

October 17th. The morning found us camped on the top of the Coteaus with no sign of Colonel Marshall and his men. Struck tents before daylight and were on the march without breakfast. At about two miles from the last camp we arrived at the Big Sioux River (here very narrow, with marshy banks), and halted for breakfast; but there was no feed for the horses. The men of the Third Regiment dealt out their last crackers, and Company G had one ration of flour, sugar, and coffee. Flour mixed with water and fried in fat was indeed and in truth a great luxury, of which even a white plumed knight might well be proud,—at this stage of the game.

The expedition was now four days' march from Camp Release, and the provisions were all gone. The scouts returned and reported that they had seen "nothing of Marshall or any other man." We again resumed the march, and at sundown arrived at Hawk's Nest Lake. Here we met Quinn (the scout), and some mounted men, who brought the cheering news of the capture of 150 Indians, including 34 warriors.

On leaving the main body of the expedition, Colonel Marshall had moved forward as rapidly as possible, and soon after midnight on the 17th overtook and surrounded the Indians, who, not anticipating such an event, were camped down and peacefully enjoying a good night's rest. The baying of their dogs was the first intimation that they had of the presence of the troops. The scouts informed them that they would not be harmed, and demanded their immediate surrender, which was complied with. A few of the younger men attempted to get away, but were overtaken and all made prisoners. By this capture much stolen property, in the way of goods, oxen, horses, and wagons, was recovered.

Only one white child was found among them. The prisoners (warriors) were brought in under guard, their weapons having been taken from them, and they were securely tied. Among them was one chief, Wa-ka-mo-no (Wa-kan-mane), Spirit Walker, or Walking Spirit. At 10 p.m. William Quinn and two mounted men were dispatched to Camp Release to obtain a reinforcement to meet the expedition with provisions and forage.

In honour of the successful termination of the pursuit and capture of the Indians, Colonel Marshall changed the name of Hawk's Nest Lake [2] to Captive Lake. The lake is very long, winding, and deep, and was very high, trees standing in the water 12 feet from the shore. Very singularly it rises and falls without any apparent assistance from the rains or snows, as if it had a connection with some underground system of streams.

· October 18th. According to the estimates of the scouts and others we were about 120 miles from Camp Release and 25 miles from James River, or half way between the Big Sioux and the James. Left Captive Lake bright and early, and halted on the Big Sioux for dinner, at the place where we breakfasted (?) the day previous. Took coffee with the Third Regiment. At the request of Major Brown, we took his sister-in-law (a squaw by the name of Sinte, the wife of Captain James

2. This lake is probably the most eastern one of the two lakes now known as Twin Lakes, situated in township 118 north, of range 54 west, in Coddington county, South Dakota, as no other lake in this region corresponds with the description. Its Dakota name is Chan-nonpa (Two Wood Lake), and that of the western one is Tizaptona (Five Lodge Lake). "Wild Goose Nest" (Magaiticage) and "Hawk's Nest" (Hecaoti) Lakes are "on the Minnesota Coteaus," and not over thirty miles west of the state line.—T. H. L.

Gorman of the Renville Rangers) into our wagon. In order to have a little fun as a side diversion, a race with our mules was commenced, the tailor George driving. His position was lubricous as he drove over the rough ground, shaking the squaw and the old man well. Having gotten some distance ahead, we halted at a creek for target practice; and some good shots were made.

Homeward bound, as viewed from a high ridge, the appearance of our train was romantic and picturesque. The Indian warriors with their mounted guard were in the advance, and then the infantry with their arms and bayonets shining brightly. The mounted men with their Sharps rifles, contrasting with the Springfields carried by Company G; then comes the "little barker" (the mountain howitzer on wheels in a wagon), the gunners riding alongside; then our teams laden with camp equipage, tents, kettles, etc., the whole cavalcade ending with the Indian camp following in true Indian style. Ponies loaded almost to the ground: cows, oxen and wagons the same; and squaws loaded as if their backs would break. A pretty squaw, with a snow-white blanket around her, is perched high on top of a big load on a little pony; then there are other ponies with *papooses* on their backs, followed by any quantity of dogs.

A simple strap is thrown across the back of a pony, ox, or cow, supporting the ends of two poles, while the other ends drag on the ground; midway between the ends are perched the *tepee* skin, camp traps, etc., and on top of the whole are placed the children, who are riding as gaily as if they were on a honeymoon; a string of bells around the pony's neck, with the bellowing of the cattle, the bright blue sky above, the surrounding hills (some black with burnt grass, others green and waving), with the beautiful lakes contrasted,—combined to make it one of the strangest, wildest, and most beautiful and romantic pictures I ever witnessed. Camped at sundown on a creek between two high hills, where a cow was shot,—a promise of fresh beef for tomorrow.

Sunday, October 19th. It was cold sleeping last night; water frozen in canteen; but the day was ushered in with the sun shining bright. Breaking camp in the valley was a beautiful sight, as viewed from the top of the adjoining hill,—fires burning, tents taken down, mounted men starting off at a brisk trot. Infantry looked lively and cheerful at the prospect of soon greeting their comrades at Camp Release, with their good success, prisoners, spoils, etc., they march straight up the hill, while the teams and "Moccasin Train" wind around the sides to make the ascent more easy. Such a scene as here witnessed carries one back to the days when he read fancy sketches of such expeditions in novels. With a party of friends we were now in advance of the train, and during the day shot geese, brant, ducks and snipes. It was indeed a grand sight to see thousands of white brant flying between us and the burned and blackened hills.

Arrived at our old camp "Hollow" at the head of the Lac qui Parle at 3 p.m.,—one hour in advance of the train,—and took advantage of the occasion to cook and feast on some of our game. The train arrived, having in charge more prisoners, who had been out hunting, and, on returning and finding their band all gone, followed our trail and gave themselves up.

October 20th. More Indians joined us last night; they attempted to slip in past the guard, but were caught. Struck tents at daylight and resumed the march, crossing the line into Minnesota at 10 a.m. Met the relief train under Quinn at 11 a.m. After leaving Captive Lake, and at a point some 18 miles distant, William Quinn's horse gave out, and was abandoned. He walked all the rest of the way to Camp Release beside of the other horses, reaching there at 11 o'clock Saturday night (making good time). He took a short nap, started on the return trip Sunday morning, and met the train as above stated. He brought the news of the capture of 23 more lodges (67 Indians) near the lower Lac qui Parle by Captain Merriman and a detachment of the Sixth Regiment, who took them to Camp Release.

At 12 o'clock, noon, we arrived at the camping place first used on our outward trip. Took dinner with the artillery. The prairie took fire from Company G's cook-fire, making us skedaddle at a double-quick. The flames spread with fearful rapidity, causing consternation and alarm, and inducing the moccasin train to move at a lively gait. There was a feeling of real joy when all had reached burned ground. Quinn now led us by a new route. The prairie was on fire all around us, and at one point we passed between two fires. The camp for the night was established on a beautiful spot near the bank of the Lac qui Parle River. Was appointed officer of the guard.

During the night there were indications of the prisoners trying to escape. C. J. Sudheimer and Peter Molitor were placed as sentinels on the top of the edge of the plateau, near the camp. The wind was blowing at a 30 or 35 mile gait, so they finally took post on the more sheltered slope near the top. About 11 p.m. an Indian with a halter in his hand appeared and crossed the line some 50 feet distant, when he was halted by Sudheimer, who, finding that he was a prisoner trying to make his escape, promptly arrested him.

I immediately doubled the guard and had all the prisoners (warriors) searched, which resulted in the finding of a pocket-knife, which was duly confiscated. The job of searching them was very disagreeable. Ugh! what filth. This task being completed, they were securely tied, placed in a Sibley tent, and a double guard stationed over them. Visited the Indian camp with George Brown to see the sights. Found them in their *tepees* spread out around the fire, which was located in the centre.

October 21st. Broke camp before daybreak, and was on the march before sunrise. The day proved to be a horrible one, the wind blowing a perfect hurricane; the black dust of the burnt prairie filling and blinding our eyes, the lashes on which the dust accumulated creating a cutting, grinding pain, causing us to suffer much pain. Being near our journey's end, we moved forward as fast as it was possible under the circumstances, and arrived at Camp Release at 4 p.m., where we joined our comrades, who were very glad to see us. But our arrival did not improve matters so far as we were concerned, for the camp was a perfect wreck,—tents ripped up and chimneys blown down. There was not much news at the camp, the most important event during our absence having been the arrival of the sutler, on which occasion nearly all hands got tight, with the result that one colonel, six captains, and any quantity of lieutenants were put under arrest.

With all our forced marches, cold nights, windy days, and fasting, the trip was a most successful one; for, besides those who voluntarily surrendered themselves, we captured 39 men and 100 women and children, not to mention the horses, cattle, wagons, and plunder, which were also brought in.

LEONAUR

ALSO FROM LEONAUR
AVAILABLE IN SOFTCOVER OR HARDCOVER WITH DUST JACKET

THE 2ND MAORI WAR: 1860-1861 *by Robert Carey*—The Second Maori War, or First Taranaki War, one more bloody instalment of the conflicts between European settlers and the indigenous Maori people.

A JOURNAL OF THE SECOND SIKH WAR *by Daniel A. Sandford*—The Experiences of an Ensign of the 2nd Bengal European Regiment During the Campaign in the Punjab, India, 1848-49.

THE LIGHT INFANTRY OFFICER *by John H. Cooke*—The Experiences of an Officer of the 43rd Light Infantry in America During the War of 1812.

BUSHVELDT CARBINEERS *by George Witton*—The War Against the Boers in South Africa and the 'Breaker' Morant Incident.

LAKE'S CAMPAIGNS IN INDIA *by Hugh Pearse*—The Second Anglo Maratha War, 1803-1807.

BRITAIN IN AFGHANISTAN 1: THE FIRST AFGHAN WAR 1839-42 *by Archibald Forbes*—From invasion to destruction-a British military disaster.

BRITAIN IN AFGHANISTAN 2: THE SECOND AFGHAN WAR 1878-80 *by Archibald Forbes*—This is the history of the Second Afghan War-another episode of British military history typified by savagery, massacre, siege and battles.

UP AMONG THE PANDIES *by Vivian Dering Majendie*—Experiences of a British Officer on Campaign During the Indian Mutiny, 1857-1858.

MUTINY: 1857 *by James Humphries*—Authentic Voices from the Indian Mutiny-First Hand Accounts of Battles, Sieges and Personal Hardships.

BLOW THE BUGLE, DRAW THE SWORD *by W. H. G. Kingston*—The Wars, Campaigns, Regiments and Soldiers of the British & Indian Armies During the Victorian Era, 1839-1898.

WAR BEYOND THE DRAGON PAGODA *by Major J. J. Snodgrass*—A Personal Narrative of the First Anglo-Burmese War 1824 - 1826.

THE HERO OF ALIWAL *by James Humphries*—The Campaigns of Sir Harry Smith in India, 1843-1846, During the Gwalior War & the First Sikh War.

ALL FOR A SHILLING A DAY *by Donald F. Featherstone*—The story of H.M. 16th, the Queen's Lancers During the first Sikh War 1845-1846.

LEONAUR

ALSO FROM LEONAUR
AVAILABLE IN SOFTCOVER OR HARDCOVER WITH DUST JACKET

ADVENTURES OF A YOUNG RIFLEMAN *by Johann Christian Maempel*—The Experiences of a Saxon in the French & British Armies During the Napoleonic Wars.

THE HUSSAR *by Norbert Landsheit & G. R. Gleig*—A German Cavalryman in British Service Throughout the Napoleonic Wars.

RECOLLECTIONS OF THE PENINSULA *by Moyle Sherer*—An Officer of the 34th Regiment of Foot—'The Cumberland Gentlemen'—on Campaign Against Napoleon's French Army in Spain.

MARINE OF REVOLUTION & CONSULATE *by Moreau de Jonnès*—The Recollections of a French Soldier of the Revolutionary Wars 1791-1804.

GENTLEMEN IN RED *by John Dobbs & Robert Knowles*—Two Accounts of British Infantry Officers During the Peninsular War Recollections of an Old 52nd Man by John Dobbs An Officer of Fusiliers by Robert Knowles.

CORPORAL BROWN'S CAMPAIGNS IN THE LOW COUNTRIES *by Robert Brown*—Recollections of a Coldstream Guard in the Early Campaigns Against Revolutionary France 1793-1795.

THE 7TH (QUEENS OWN) HUSSARS: Volume 2—1793-1815 *by C. R. B. Barrett*—During the Campaigns in the Low Countries & the Peninsula and Waterloo Campaigns of the Napoleonic Wars. Volume 2: 1793-1815.

THE MARENGO CAMPAIGN 1800 *by Herbert H. Sargent*—The Victory that Completed the Austrian Defeat in Italy.

DONALDSON OF THE 94TH—SCOTS BRIGADE *by Joseph Donaldson*—The Recollections of a Soldier During the Peninsula & South of France Campaigns of the Napoleonic Wars.

A CONSCRIPT FOR EMPIRE *by Philippe as told to Johann Christian Maempel*—The Experiences of a Young German Conscript During the Napoleonic Wars.

JOURNAL OF THE CAMPAIGN OF 1815 *by Alexander Cavalié Mercer*—The Experiences of an Officer of the Royal Horse Artillery During the Waterloo Campaign.

NAPOLEON'S CAMPAIGNS IN POLAND 1806-7 *by Robert Wilson*—The campaign in Poland from the Russian side of the conflict.

LEONAUR

ALSO FROM LEONAUR

AVAILABLE IN SOFTCOVER OR HARDCOVER WITH DUST JACKET

BUGEAUD: A PACK WITH A BATON *by Thomas Robert Bugeaud*—The Early Campaigns of a Soldier of Napoleon's Army Who Would Become a Marshal of France.

WATERLOO RECOLLECTIONS *by Frederick Llewellyn*—Rare First Hand Accounts, Letters, Reports and Retellings from the Campaign of 1815.

SERGEANT NICOL *by Daniel Nicol*—The Experiences of a Gordon Highlander During the Napoleonic Wars in Egypt, the Peninsula and France.

THE JENA CAMPAIGN: 1806 *by F. N. Maude*—The Twin Battles of Jena & Auerstadt Between Napoleon's French and the Prussian Army.

PRIVATE O'NEIL *by Charles O'Neil*—The recollections of an Irish Rogue of H. M. 28th Regt.—The Slashers—during the Peninsula & Waterloo campaigns of the Napoleonic war.

ROYAL HIGHLANDER *by James Anton*—A soldier of H.M 42nd (Royal) Highlanders during the Peninsular, South of France & Waterloo Campaigns of the Napoleonic Wars.

CAPTAIN BLAZE *by Elzéar Blaze*—Life in Napoleons Army.

LEJEUNE VOLUME 1 *by Louis-François Lejeune*—The Napoleonic Wars through the Experiences of an Officer on Berthier's Staff.

LEJEUNE VOLUME 2 *by Louis-François Lejeune*—The Napoleonic Wars through the Experiences of an Officer on Berthier's Staff.

CAPTAIN COIGNET *by Jean-Roch Coignet*—A Soldier of Napoleon's Imperial Guard from the Italian Campaign to Russia and Waterloo.

FUSILIER COOPER *by John S. Cooper*—Experiences in the 7th (Royal) Fusiliers During the Peninsular Campaign of the Napoleonic Wars and the American Campaign to New Orleans.

FIGHTING NAPOLEON'S EMPIRE *by Joseph Anderson*—The Campaigns of a British Infantryman in Italy, Egypt, the Peninsular & the West Indies During the Napoleonic Wars.

CHASSEUR BARRES *by Jean-Baptiste Barres*—The experiences of a French Infantryman of the Imperial Guard at Austerlitz, Jena, Eylau, Friedland, in the Peninsular, Lutzen, Bautzen, Zinnwald and Hanau during the Napoleonic Wars.

LEONAUR

ALSO FROM LEONAUR
AVAILABLE IN SOFTCOVER OR HARDCOVER WITH DUST JACKET

THE LIFE OF THE REAL BRIGADIER GERARD VOLUME 1—THE YOUNG HUSSAR 1782-1807 *by Jean-Baptiste De Marbot*—A French Cavalryman Of the Napoleonic Wars at Marengo, Austerlitz, Jena, Eylau & Friedland.

THE LIFE OF THE REAL BRIGADIER GERARD VOLUME 2—IMPERIAL AIDE-DE-CAMP 1807-1811 *by Jean-Baptiste De Marbot*—A French Cavalryman of the Napoleonic Wars at Saragossa, Landshut, Eckmuhl, Ratisbon, Aspern-Essling, Wagram, Busaco & Torres Vedras.

THE LIFE OF THE REAL BRIGADIER GERARD VOLUME 3—COLONEL OF CHASSEURS 1811-1815 *by Jean-Baptiste De Marbot*—A French Cavalryman in the retreat from Moscow, Lutzen, Bautzen, Katzbach, Leipzig, Hanau & Waterloo.

THE INDIAN WAR OF 1864 *by Eugene Ware*—The Experiences of a Young Officer of the 7th Iowa Cavalry on the Western Frontier During the Civil War.

THE MARCH OF DESTINY *by Charles E. Young & V. Devinny*—Dangers of the Trail in 1865 by Charles E. Young & The Story of a Pioneer by V. Devinny, two Accounts of Early Emigrants to Colorado.

CROSSING THE PLAINS *by William Audley Maxwell*—A First Hand Narrative of the Early Pioneer Trail to California in 1857.

CHIEF OF SCOUTS *by William F. Drannan*—A Pilot to Emigrant and Government Trains, Across the Plains of the Western Frontier.

THIRTY-ONE YEARS ON THE PLAINS AND IN THE MOUNTAINS *by William F. Drannan*—William Drannan was born to be a pioneer, hunter, trapper and wagon train guide during the momentous days of the Great American West.

THE INDIAN WARS VOLUNTEER *by William Thompson*—Recollections of the Conflict Against the Snakes, Shoshone, Bannocks, Modocs and Other Native Tribes of the American North West.

THE 4TH TENNESSEE CAVALRY *by George B. Guild*—The Services of Smith's Regiment of Confederate Cavalry by One of its Officers.

COLONEL WORTHINGTON'S SHILOH *by T. Worthington*—The Tennessee Campaign, 1862, by an Officer of the Ohio Volunteers.

FOUR YEARS IN THE SADDLE *by W. L. Curry*—The History of the First Regiment Ohio Volunteer Cavalry in the American Civil War.

9 780857 061058